Eating Local in the Fraser Valley

Eating Local

in the **Fraser Valley**

A Food-Lover's Guide, Featuring Over 70 Recipes from Farmers, Producers, and Chefs

By Angie Quaale

Foreword by Karen Barnaby
Photography by Ric Ernst · Illustrations by Kay Slater

appetite
by RANDOM HOUSE

Library and Archives of Canada Cataloguing in Publication is available upon request.

ISBN: 978-0-14-753031-8

eBook ISBN: 978-0-14-753032-5

Cover and book photography by Ric Ernst

Author photo by Jennifer Kirk

Illustrations by Kay Slater

Watercolor art on page v by Cilla Watts

Additional photography on pages 6, 15, 58, 59, and inside front and back cover by Gojoy; on pages 25, 88 and 89 by Chuck Russell

Printed and bound in China

Published by Appetite by Random House®,

a division of Penguin Random House Canada Limited.

www.penguinrandomhouse.ca

10 9 8 7 6 5 4 3 2 1

appetite
by RANDOM HOUSE

Penguin
Random
House

This book is for all the people who aren't afraid to get their hands dirty.
And to my parents, all of them—Mom and Dave, Dad and Cilla—
I hit the family lottery with you and am grateful every day that you taught me to be grateful.

Contents

Foreword

If you follow what's happening in food, you'll know the focus is usually on big cities, big chefs, and big events. Everyone is consumed with the bigness, the competitions, the best "whatever-is-fashionable-this-month" that also happens to be miles away from where they actually live. We have big and small screens that allow instant access to the world of food. On one hand, if it's not on a screen, it's not there. On the other hand, our screens have pointed out the disconnect between what we choose to put in our mouths and where it comes from. And if you really follow what's happening in food, you'll know that change is happening: praise and focus are moving to the family-run farm, the cheesemakers, and the small meat shop that has been making sausages the same way for 50 years. It's almost like food is getting back to its roots. The farmers and producers are serving the community that surrounds them, the way they used to—and the way it should be.

Short of actually growing food yourself, the next best thing is knowing the people who have pulled the carrot out of the ground, made the cheese from the animals you can see grazing in the field, or made the wine from the grapes growing right over *there*.

Angie Quaale has all this knowledge, and for as long as I've known her, she's been an influencer and connector, a champion of all the good things that the Fraser Valley has to offer. I will admit that I snobbishly thought it was odd at first, until I realized that, yes, this is where most of our outstanding local food and beverages come from. I should have smacked myself, because I was the person who was thinking small while Angie was thinking big. You can feel and taste her enthusiasm by merely leafing through this book.

I know it's unusual to describe a cookbook as a "page turner." This book is so engaging that I was eager to see what was on the next page, and I was never disappointed. Did you know that there is a rice paddy that provides rice to an artisan sake maker, a farm that grows fresh goji berries, and an orchard that grows 60 varieties of apples? Or that there are multiple cheesemakers and wineries in this abundant valley?

Angie has opened the doors to a wonderful array of producers, beverage makers, and chefs in the Fraser Valley, and she provides recipes to help you make the best use of all the delicious ingredients and products they offer. The recipes are accessible, well written, and easy to follow. Do you want a champion burger recipe for your next BBQ? It's in here. Never-Fail Pastry, Dutch Sour Wit Caramel Sauce, and Fresh Cheese Curd Panzanella Salad should also be on your list of recipes to try. And for those who enjoy creative cocktails, there are outstanding ones in these pages.

If you love food, do yourself a big favor and plan a few day trips using this book as a guide. Stock up, find a nice spot to have a picnic, or go to one of the great restaurants that Angie praises. Take your children to a berry farm and show them that the berries come from plants and let them get all messy with ripe berries; take them to a dairy farm and show them that milk comes from cows, goats, and sheep and that it all can be made into butter and cheese.

Put away your screens for a day, feel the sun, smell the earth, and listen to the trees rustling in the breeze and the birds chirping. Experience the bigness, and settle into this wonderful world that Angie has opened up for you.

—Karen Barnaby

Introduction

In southwestern BC, tucked between Vancouver and Hope and just north of the US border, is a gem of an area called the Fraser Valley. The geographical definition of the region is a little fluid—you'll find that many locals have their own ideas about where the boundaries lie—but "my" Fraser Valley includes the areas of (from west to east) Surrey, Langley, Abbotsford, and Chilliwack, with Mission, Pitt Meadows, and Maple Ridge to the north. Those are not the official boundaries, but that is my definition for the purposes of this book.

The Fraser Valley is an incredibly beautiful, diverse, and constantly changing region—and it's popular too. It's one of the most rapidly growing regions in Canada, with about 3 million people currently calling it home. Yet despite the number of residents, there's a sense of freedom and space. That might be due to the combination of rural and urban areas that exist happily side by side. All I know is that it works.

The very best way to experience the Fraser Valley is in person, often. It's a place you need to visit, explore, and discover—and the good news is that doing that might be some of the best time you have ever spent. Each season has its own distinct flavor and feel—buzzing bees and the scent of spring flowers signal that winter is finally over; the unmistakable smell of freshly cut grass lingers in the background during lazy days at the lake, afternoon BBQs by the river, and long, warm summer nights; crisp fall breezes nudge you along during trips to the pumpkin patch and to farmers markets to shop for root vegetables; and occasional snowstorms set the scene for snowshoeing trips followed by homemade hot chocolate and a delicious bowl of soup to take off the chill. There are great reasons to visit quite literally every day. The hardest part will be deciding how long you can stay! Take a day trip, spend the weekend, or spend a week—there is always plenty to do.

The drive through the Fraser Valley (or the Valley, as locals call it) is easy and can be quite leisurely, and the cities are very clearly identified with great signage, although the municipal boundaries seamlessly blend into one another: Surrey flows into Langley, which flows into Abbotsford, which flows into Chilliwack, so don't be limited by a map. They are all so close together, so easily accessible from Highway 1, that you can pop in and out of several or all of them in a single trip. No matter which direction you arrive from, the landscape is utterly distracting—the hills and mountains beckon you, drawing you in and embracing you, leaving you in doubt that you're in a real valley; the lush fields will give you pause to appreciate the benefits of the rain that locals so often tire of in winter; and the creeks and rivers display a unique combination of nature's power and calm. If you're a city dweller, it will feel like entering another world. Don't be surprised if you find yourself breathing slowly and deeply, savoring every second of your drive.

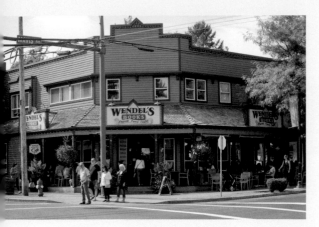

You won't need a passport to cross the bridge across the Fraser River, and you don't need any special shoes (although rubber boots might serve you well), but you do need a sense of adventure, a minor sense of direction (remember, the Coast Mountains, home of the famous Golden Ears peaks, are always to your north), and most importantly, a good appetite—because, for me, the best thing about the Fraser Valley is the food. In fact, the Fraser Valley is the heart of food production and, increasingly, beer, wine, and cider production, for the Lower Mainland of BC. It is full of dedicated, creative, and inspiring farmers, food and beverage producers, and chefs, as well as a community that supports eating local.

This book is meant to entice you to spend time in the Fraser Valley. To encourage you to visit the area and get to know the producers, farmers, and chefs of the region and experience in person their passion for the food and beverages they produce. The list of people and places I could have included in this book is endless, so I've tried to give a good overview of what's on offer. In the end, the folks and food featured in this book are all personally important to me, based on experiences I've had and relationships I've formed, and I hope you enjoy getting to know them too.

Email: angie@wellseasoned.ca
Facebook: @QuaaleAngie
Instagram: angiequaale
Twitter: @AngieQuaale

If you're a visitor to the region, I hope this book inspires you to fall in love with the Fraser Valley and to stay, play, eat, drink, and enjoy everything this incredible region has to offer. If you're a local, the chances are good that it will introduce you to a place or a person you have never heard of before and encourage you to explore more of the area you are lucky enough to call home.

As you explore the Fraser Valley, you will discover new places—not least because somewhere new seems to open every week! Please feel free to share your experiences and discoveries with me. I would love nothing more than to hear about your adventures (see the sidebar above for ways to reach me).

Fraser Valley Food

I've lived in the Fraser Valley for almost 25 years, and I can't imagine living anywhere else. My other half, David, and I live in the Township of Langley. That's where I proudly serve as an elected municipal councillor and run my business, Well Seasoned, a gourmet food store that sprang from my love of good food and my belief in the importance of supporting local food producers. I opened Well Seasoned because I saw large food companies edging independent producers off the shelf (literally). So much of what is sold right now in our supermarkets is made by the same companies in the same factories with the same ingredients and is trucked around the world to cookie-cutter multinational stores, leaving us with far fewer choices than we even realize. When I opened Well Seasoned, my main goal was to sell things you couldn't get at the regular grocery store. I wanted to offer my customers a diversity of small-batch, locally made, interesting artisan food that the grocery stores don't offer anymore. I wanted to give customers back their choice, and I wanted to provide small-scale, independent producers with an outlet to reach customers, share their stories, and have their visions championed. You may not be surprised to learn that Well Seasoned is a sponsor of the Circle Farm Tour (circlefarmtour.com). (If you've ever participated in the Circle Farm Tour, you might recognize some of the names in this book.)

My appreciation for food started when I was very young. Food was how we spoke to each other when I was growing up. My family had dinner together every night at the kitchen table. Some nights it was just a grilled cheese sandwich before we ran out the door to a softball practice or a dance recital, but we always shared a meal.

On nights when there was nowhere to be, we would sit at the table trading stories of our day until eventually someone, usually me, was laughing so hard that milk was coming out of their nose. My mom was a good cook. Not a chef, but a good cook who knows the importance of a family meal. Her mom was a bit less of a good cook, but she also knew that if you wanted the family together, you called them to the dinner table. She knew food was what got them to the table, but it wasn't the reason they stayed. This is where my love of dinner at the table came from. Sharing a meal, for me, is a big deal. It means taking time away from everything else, as important or necessary as those things may be, to sit down with someone and connect. Enjoying the company of the people you're with, breaking bread, and savoring that *time*, that is what's important. The food doesn't have to be elaborate—a simple croissant and hot coffee, or a lingering lunch or wine-fueled dinner are equally satisfying—but the quality and origin of the food I prepare and share with my loved ones do matter to me.

Eating Locally and Seasonally

Fresh, local, peak-of-the-season produce, regardless of the season, is what I love most. But shopping local is an investment on several levels. Taking the time to find out the source of your food is a luxury most of us can't accommodate every day, myself included, but somehow, when I know where my food comes from, it always tastes better. There can be so much satisfaction in understanding how your food got to your table and knowing that the people who grew it did it because they respect the earth, the environment, the process, and, ultimately, the people they grow it for.

Of course, I do buy some imported food, but I try to limit myself to those things that can't be grown, or grown in a sustainable manner, locally—and I make a point of buying these products from local, independent outlets. Seasonal produce, the best-quality olive oil, fresh lemons, spices, and grains from all over the world, local cheese and protein, and delicious BC wine is a winning combination every time at my house. Oh, and coffee, don't forget the coffee. It's always imported, but locally roasted. (Talk about getting the best of both worlds!)

We have choices, lots of them, and as a consumer, your wallet is your strongest bargaining chip. Choosing to buy local will have a far-reaching influence, probably more than you can imagine.

Eating Local, Wherever You Are

When we support our local farmers, producers, growers, and artisans, we empower them to continue to do what they do best. Buying local food is one of the most important investments we can make.

• **Local food supports local families.** The wholesale prices that farmers get for their products are low, often near the cost of production. Local farmers who sell direct to consumers cut out the middlemen and get paid full retail price for their food—which helps farm families stay on the land, continue to grow their business, and provide us with choices in our food supply. When farmers get paid fairly for their work, they are less likely to sell farmland for development, preserving it for future generations. This is exactly why farmers love to sell at farmers markets and why it is so important to support them there.

• **Locally grown food is picked at its peak.** It doesn't have to sit in the back of a truck for several days to get to you, and farmers can actually let the food ripen before they pick it, which is why it also tastes better.

• **Local livestock is processed in small-scale, local facilities.** The farmer has a relationship with the processors, overseeing and ensuring quality through the whole process.

• **Local food is good for the environment.** Well-managed farms conserve fertile soil, protect our aquifers and waterways, and provide habitat for wildlife in our communities. I really believe that customers want to support local farmers and producers and are actually willing to pay a little more to do so. That's why places here in the Fraser Valley—like Bonetti Meats, 1 Fish 2 Fish, and Well Seasoned—that are willing to buy food for a fair price, sell food for a fair price, and explain it rather than apologize for it are infinitely important to the farmer/consumer relationship.

So, if you don't have time to visit the farms as often as you'd like, I encourage you to have a conversation with the people who sell you your food. Do they share your food values? Can they tell you where your food is coming from? If not, keep talking until you find someone who can.

To me, the seasonality of the food is crucial. Buying Mexican strawberries in November feels counterintuitive. If we eat what is available when it is available locally, like we did when I was a kid, I'm sure we would all be better for it. I don't ever remember eating peaches in February unless they were the ones my family canned. There is something to be said for the renewed interest in preserving our food. It's easier and less laborious than most expect, and it is so incredibly rewarding. We teach classes on canning and preserving at Well Seasoned, and the people who take the classes are amazed at how simple it is, how affordable it is, and how incredibly rewarding it is to be able to enjoy, all year long, the seasonal food bounty that was harvested fresh at its peak. Interestingly, it's the "younger generation" (ha ha—that is, anyone younger than me) that is picking up the sealing rings and learning about preserving. They're wanting to get back to basics, eat fewer preservatives, and have better access to local food all year. This makes me very happy!

Producers, Farmers, and Chefs

Of course, none of this would happen without a very special group of people. In this book I am proud to introduce you to my friends—the farmers, the chefs, the families, and the assorted other folks—who produce the food and beverages of the Fraser Valley and play with them, reimagine them, and use them to fuel their passion. I want you to know a bit about how they ended up where they are today, where their passion or ideas came from, and how they decided to feed our world. I am fascinated by their connection to their community and their customers and by what makes them want to keep doing what they do.

The people behind the food in the Fraser Valley are as diverse as the produce of the region itself. Some local farmers are third- or fourth-generation, while others are new immigrants and brand-new hobby farmers. It's an amazing blend of history, tradition, and evolution, all resulting in some of the tastiest food and beverages you'll find anywhere in Canada. Every time I visit a farm, I leave with a deeper sense of appreciation for the people who work the land. I couldn't do it. I don't want to do it. But wow, am I ever grateful they do. Farming, I think, has to be somewhere in your DNA. Farmers farm for the love of farming, to watch and nurture their crops, to be outdoors! They love that they get to live where they work and to work where they live. The ones I know best love the independence a farm life provides, and it is just that—a life, not a lifestyle. As for the producers, in the years I have been running Well Seasoned, I have met some pretty amazing people. I have seen some companies grow and thrive, while others are happy to stay small and independent because they know scaling up their product sometimes changes the integrity of it, and the integrity of the product is why they started. For that, all of those folks have my undying admiration.

In this book you'll discover the farm-to-plate philosophies of the chefs and farmers as well as the field-to-glass philosophies of the winemakers, beer brewers, and cidermakers. I have the utmost appreciation for the creativity and individuality behind their food and drinks. I can't imagine living in a world where this level of creativity and individuality didn't exist. I feel so lucky to live in a region and a climate where they are embraced and fostered. But creativity and individuality can thrive only if the people behind them are supported, appreciated, and ultimately empowered to earn a good living. Talk to any of the producers you meet along the way; they will be very happy to share a story or two about what shopping locally means to them. Having all of this

The People Behind Your Food

There are three numbers everyone should have on speed dial: your parents' (obviously), a butcher's, and a fishmonger's. I don't think I need to say anything about your parents. You know who they are and what happens when you don't call! So let's look at the next two people on the list.

I have a butcher whom I trust implicitly. His name is Carlo Bonetti. He owns Bonetti Meats, a second-generation meat shop in Langley. His father, Italo, came from Italy and started the business in 1973. Bonetti Meats has grown and evolved over the years. Ownership may have passed from father to son, but the integrity of the work they do remains the same. Carlo can tell you exactly where all of the meat in his shop came from, usually the name of the guy or gal who raised it, where it was slaughtered, and how it has been processed. I know I'm getting the best he has to give every time I shop there. And now it thrills me to no end to visit the shop and see Carlo's sons, Michael and Enzo, learning the family business and excited to be experimenting with recipes of their own in the smokehouse.

I also have a fishmonger. Her name is Heather Jenkins, and she is the owner of 1 Fish 2 Fish (1fish2fish.ca) in Langley City. Heather sells only Ocean Wise seafood, and she knows exactly where everything in her shop came from, how it was caught, when it was caught, and how it has been handled. Heather's respect for the sustainability of the industry is incredible. She sells only seafood she is proud to have in her case, and that level of pride resonates through all of her staff and the business she has built. She shucks a mean oyster and can get you 100 pounds of BC wild sockeye with very little notice when you have forgotten to order it for a catering job. (Or so I have been told.)

amazing choice at our doorstep is, to me, such a privilege, one I am not prepared to give up, which is why I shop local at every opportunity. The good news is that anyone who offers that support benefits directly and immediately by consuming the wonderful end products. Is it just me, or does that sound like the ultimate win-win scenario?

Recipes

The majority of the recipes in this book have been contributed by the farmers, producers, and chefs who are featured, and the others are ones I have been making with local ingredients for years. You'll find that they not only are tasty, but also show off the best of our local produce—and, I hope, they will have you coming back to the Valley to stock up often. Of course, if I specify a certain product made by the producer in the profile and you don't have it on hand, please feel free to substitute your own favorite brand. Here are another couple of notes on the recipes to keep you on track as you cook your way through them:

- When the recipe calls for salt and pepper, my preference is for sea salt and cracked black pepper, unless otherwise specified
- Herbs are fresh, unless otherwise specified
- Vegetables and fruits are fresh, unless otherwise specified, and should be washed thoroughly before use
- Eggs are best when farm-fresh
- Sugar is granulated unless otherwise specified; brown sugar is packed
- Sour cream is full-fat; whipping cream is 35%
- Parmesan is freshly grated
- You can use any grade of maple syrup (but don't use pancake syrup)
- Orange juice and lemon juice are freshly squeezed
- Citrus zest is grated unless otherwise specified

How to Use This Book

*T*his book is laid out in chapters by region: Langley, Abbotsford, Chilliwack, and then our Neighbors (Surrey, Mission, Pitt Meadows, and Maple Ridge). Each chapter includes a map to give you an idea of the lay of the land and a general introduction to the area. The first three chapters are broken into sections of Producers, Chefs and Local Champions, and Other Places to Visit; then, because the Neighbors chapter covers four cities, I had to limit myself to just Producers and Other Places to Visit for that one.

Each producer has a number and is shown on the map to help you plan your visit, whether you're looking for a tasting experience or you're stocking up on fresh meat and produce for dinner. The chefs and local champions I've chosen to feature are those key individuals who cook, teach, write, or otherwise support the wonderful food and drink network in the Valley. And the other places to visit are some more of the fabulous spots in the Valley that are worth a trip but that I couldn't fit into the main book because of space constraints (and limiting myself to only a handful of these per chapter was nothing short of torture!).

If there is something you really want to see or do, visit their website or call before you leave home—all of the places featured in this book have seasonal hours, timed closures, special events, and visitor information that can change frequently. All of the spots I have picked are family-friendly to one degree or another, but use your common sense so that everyone can enjoy themselves.

There are farmers markets happening in almost every corner of the Fraser Valley.

Times and dates change, depending on the location and season. A quick online search will help you find local markets in the area you are touring, or you can visit the BC Association of Farmers' Markets' website (bcfarmersmarket.org), where you will find a comprehensive list of the markets in BC.

If a market isn't listed in the BCAFM website it is because it doesn't meet their criteria to be a true farmers market: To be considered a true farmers market (as opposed to a community market or artisan market), a market must be composed entirely of vendors who make, bake, grow, or raise the products they sell and a majority of those vendors must sell farm products from BC. Farmers markets are a serious business for our local farmers. That being said, you can also find some really great "stuff," and usually some local farmers and producers also selling their product at artisan or community markets, so don't pass them up too quickly. I know I find them hard to resist.

This book is not meant to be a prescription of must-sees and must-dos, as that would be such a disservice to you. My dream day is probably not your dream day (although if you like ice cream, meat, and cider, we'd probably have a great time together). Your visit needs to be personalized and customized to suit you, your tour companions, and the weather. I've included a short calendar guide (page 253) and a couple of sample itineraries (page 248), but these really are just optional starting points to give you some ideas if you feel overwhelmed by choice. I want you to visit the places that appeal most to you and to give yourself plenty of freedom to get distracted and discover new people, new places, and new produce. Don't be afraid to follow a handmade road sign, drive to get a better view of the sunset, or just get lost. You never know, you might stumble over a hidden gem—there are many of them here in this bountiful, beautiful valley.

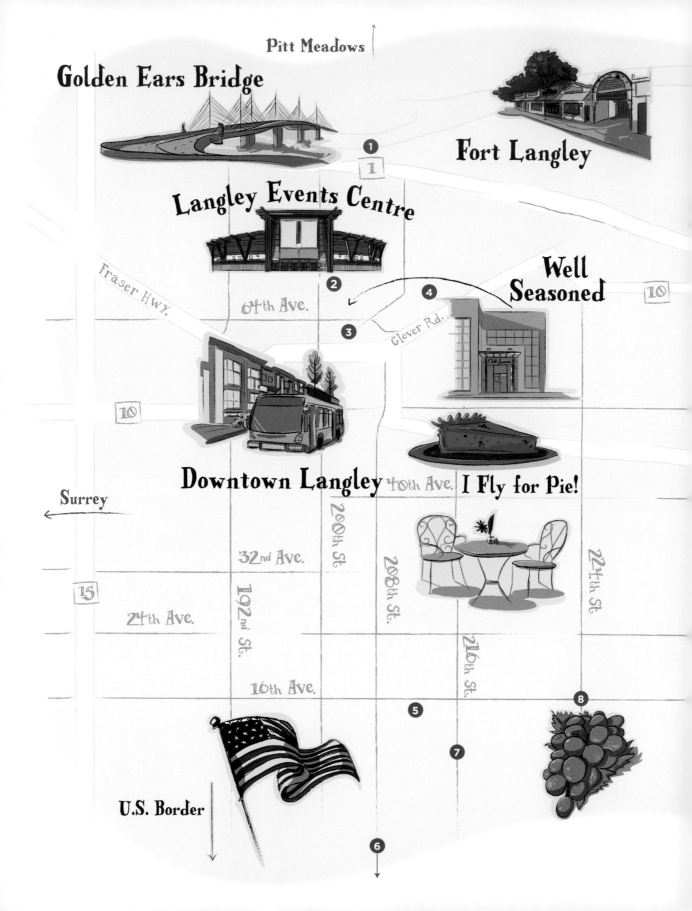

Pitt Meadows

Golden Ears Bridge

1
1

Fort Langley

Langley Events Centre

2

64th Ave.

4

Well Seasoned

10

3

Glover Rd.

Downtown Langley

40th Ave.

I Fly for Pie!

Surrey

10

15

32nd Ave.

24th Ave.

16th Ave.

200th St.

192nd St.

208th St.

216th St.

224th St.

5

7

8

6

U.S. Border

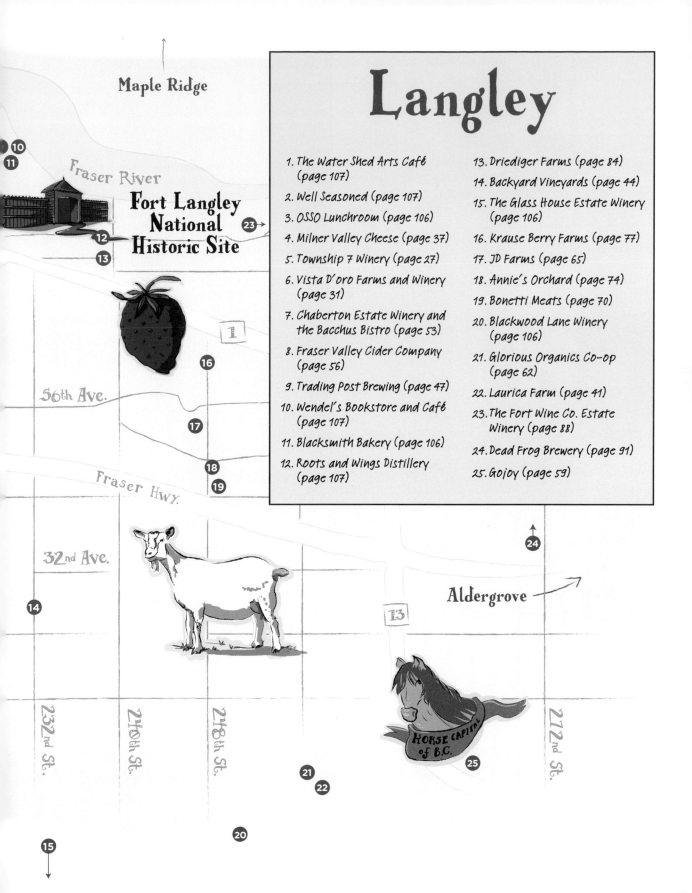

Langley

Maple Ridge

Fraser River

Fort Langley National Historic Site

56th Ave.

Fraser Hwy.

32nd Ave.

Aldergrove

HORSE CAPITAL of B.C.

232nd St.

240th St.

248th St.

272nd St.

Langley

This is my home. It is also my favorite part of the Fraser Valley for a million reasons that I think will be obvious as soon as you visit. You can almost feel the history, the charm, and the hospitality the second you set foot in the area.

Langley is the traditional territorial land of the Kwantlen, Sto:lo, and Katzie First Nations. There are two Langleys—yes, weird, I know—the Township and the City. In 1955, a referendum held in the Langley Prairie, as it was then known, resulted in a split into two separate municipalities, today's City of Langley and Township of Langley. What was the dispute? Streetlights. The businesses in the "city" wanted modern amenities and the farmers of the day didn't want to pay for them, so they split. The boundaries aren't distinct, and most people don't know if they're visiting the Township or the City of Langley, so it can get a little confusing if you're looking at a map. Essentially, the City is a 4-square-mile donut hole in the center of the 120-square-mile Township of Langley donut.

Enough about donuts, let's talk about PIE! A very famous coffee shop called I Fly for Pie relocated from Chilliwack Airport to Langley Regional Airport in 2016. Pilots have been making it a pit stop for a cup of coffee and a slice of tasty homemade pie for almost four decades. It is an institution and the pilots obviously know a good thing when they see it, so a stop at Langley Airport should be part of your itinerary. While you and your copilot finish your coffee, you can plan the rest of your visit.

Seventy-five percent of the land in the Township of Langley is designated within the Agricultural Land Reserve, dedicated as farmland, and its use is managed by the

Agricultural Land Commission. The Township is where all the farm, food, and wine production happens. The City's inner-city core is full of specialty shops, second-hand and consignment shops, thrift stores, and cafés alongside a hotel and casino. The City hosts events at McBurney Plaza, an outdoor courtyard, and in Douglas Park all year long. You can find a full list of events on the City's website (city.langley.bc.ca).

The Township of Langley is known as a community of communities, with five distinct neighborhoods, all with a very different flair. There is *so* much to see and do, it was hard to feature only a handful of producers to keep this book a manageable size. In addition, the landscape is changing every day, with new farmgates, wineries, distilleries, shops, restaurants, and breweries opening seemingly every week. At Well Seasoned, we offer different cooking classes daily, and many of them feature food and beverages produced in Langley, so we're constantly finding out about new food and drink ventures.

South of Highway 1, you can visit the shops, restaurants, and urban core of the Langleys. The farmlands in the deep south, bordering the US, are where you'll find the wineries, the cideries, and many amazing farms. As you drive through the region, you might experience a little déjà vu. That can definitely be attributed to all of the filming done in Langley—home to shows like *Bates Motel*, *Riverdale*, *Once Upon a Time*, *Cedar Cove*, *Arctic Air*, etc. You may even spot a celebrity or two!

Barely south of and just north of Highway 1 are the berry farms, the breweries, golf courses, and Fort Langley, the birthplace of BC. Fort Langley is full of quaint shops, galleries, cafés, and antique stores—it's a fantastic place to spend a few hours between farm tours. You can visit the Fort Langley National Historic Site, tour the actual fort, pan for gold, make bannock, and learn about the original fur traders of the Hudson's Bay Company. You can walk the Fort-to-Fort Trail or ride your bike and camp riverside for the weekend. You can take a haunted walk through the cemetery and town on a Grave Tales tour around Halloween, or join the Kwantlen First Nation for a historical walking tour of their territorial lands. And you will definitely want to visit the annual Cranberry Festival and the Food Truck Festival hosted by the Fort Langley Business Improvement Association. They're fantastic ways to sample local food talent.

The Township of Langley is special. The people are warm and friendly and share so much pride in the concept of "local." The pioneers who were part of the referendum in 1955 might be surprised now to see streetlights and businesses thriving all over the municipality and not just "downtown," although there are still honor boxes at farmgates for eggs, flowers, and honey. The Township has grown over the years into a thriving municipality, but it has definitely maintained its country, small-town charm. While you are here, take in a hockey or lacrosse game—the Langley Events Centre is home to the Vancouver Giants and the Vancouver Stealth. There are great pools, spray parks, and trails, and a fabulous cycling network. There is so much to see, do, eat, drink, and enjoy, you really do need to spend the weekend! The Township's website also offers information for visitors (tol.ca).

Tourist information: **tourism-langley.ca**

Facebook: **@tourismlangley**

Instagram: **@tourismlangley**

Twitter: **@TourismLangley**

Township 7 Winery

21152 — 16th Ave., Langley, V2Z 1K3; 604-532-1766
township7.com

This quaint winery is located in the beautiful South Langley countryside, an area that was called Township 7 in the 1800s. The original cottage from 1930 is still on the property.

The terroir in Langley is very similar to that of Champagne, France, which is why the fruit grown on Township 7 Winery's Langley property (they have another vineyard and tasting room on the Naramata Bench in the Okanagan, where they grow fruit for their other varietals) is generally used to produce their sparkling wine, 7 Stars. From the 5-acre property, they harvest about 8 tons of fruit, which yields about six barrels or 300 bottles of wine. People often comment that BC wine costs more than wine from elsewhere, but think about this for a second: 5 acres, 8 tons of fruit, and a *full* growing season generate 300 bottles of wine.

Township 7 has always focused on producing small-lot, high-quality wine crafted with carefully chosen, sustainably grown grapes from both of their vineyards. Winemaker Mary McDermott makes great wine, as did Bradley Cooper (no, not *that* Bradley Cooper!), the winemaker before her who set such a high standard for Township 7 and helped create their reputation for making some of the very best wine in BC with Fraser Valley fruit. Fruit harvested in Langley is being used for an "estate exclusive" sparkling wine, a true homage to the region. All of the fruit at Township 7 is hand-harvested at its peak of ripeness, hand-sorted, and then gently pressed to preserve the fruit integrity—a true labor of love. One of the labor lovers at Township 7 in Langley is general manager Jason Ocenas, the epitome of a fabulous host!

In the spring and summer the winery hosts dozens of events: check the website for a full list. You'll see that Township 7 has something for everyone, but for wine aficionados, it's *the* place to stop to stock up the cellar.

Jason's Lobster Mac and Cheese

This very decadent dish from Jason Ocenas is best served with a simple green salad and enjoyed with some of your favorite people and a few glasses of excellent Township 7 wine.

Serves 4

1 lb penne or elbow pasta

¼ cup unsalted butter

2 cloves garlic, minced

⅔ cup all-purpose flour

½ cup Township 7 chardonnay + a glass or two for the cook

4 cups whole milk

1 can (12 oz) evaporated milk

1 lb aged cheddar, grated

1 Tbsp Dijon mustard

1 tsp smoked paprika

⅛ tsp cayenne pepper

Kosher salt

3 cups lobster meat, chopped

½ cup panko breadcrumbs

3 Tbsp extra virgin olive oil

1. Preheat the oven to 350°F.

2. Cook the pasta in a pot of boiling salted water until al dente. Drain but do not rinse.

3. Melt the butter in a large saucepan over medium heat. Add the garlic and stir for a few minutes until the garlic is soft and aromatic. Add the flour and stir until it forms a roux. Slowly add the wine as you take a sip of your own glass to appreciate the flavor of the wine. Continue to stir, incorporating the wine into the roux until smooth. Add both types of milk and whisk until smooth. Whisk in the cheese, mustard, paprika, cayenne, and a generous ½ tsp salt, continuing to whisk until everything is incorporated and the sauce is smooth. Finally, add the lobster meat, stir to combine, and pour over the cooked pasta, mixing until all the pasta is coated.

4. Pour the cheese sauce and pasta into a 9- × 13-inch baking dish, sprinkle with the breadcrumbs, and drizzle with the olive oil. Bake until the sauce is bubbly and the breadcrumbs are toasty, about 30 minutes.

5. Remove from the oven and serve immediately with more wine.

Vista D'oro Farms and Winery

346 – 208th St., Langley, V2Z 1T6; 604-514-3539
vistadoro.com

Vista D'oro Farms and Winery is an absolute oasis, almost as far south as you can go in Langley. The Murphys have 10 stunning acres of property overlooking Campbell Valley Regional Park and the Golden Ears mountain peaks. Vista D'oro has three very distinct yet complementary parts of the business: the farm, the winery, and the Preservatory. Patrick and Chef Lee Murphy farm together, growing heritage varieties of grapes, apples, pears, plums, cherries, crabapples, tomatoes, and walnuts. Patrick makes the wine and runs the winery, and Lee makes the preserves and runs the Preservatory (hence her nickname, "Jam Master Lee").

In the winery, you'll find wine made from fruit grown on the property and on Vancouver Island. Patrick's D'oro, a rich, fortified walnut wine, is the flagship offering. Made in small batches from a blend of marechal foch, merlot, and cabernet franc, Fraser Valley green walnuts, and Okanagan brandy, it spends over a year relaxing in French and American oak barrels. And when Patrick says it is ready, it is bottled and sold as one of the most unique products being made in the region.

Meanwhile, in the Preservatory, Chef Lee takes peak-of-the-season fruit, veggies, herbs, and spices and adds Vista D'oro wines to create some of the most delicious artisan preserves in the country, including her signature item: Figs and Walnut Wine preserves, made with walnuts from the 100-year-old walnut trees on the property and Patrick's D'oro. (The figs are imported.)

Patrick and Lee are hoping that when you visit them on the farm, you'll be encouraged to slow down a little. Take your time to sip some wine, enjoy a picnic on the grass, engage in some good conversation, and just bask in the surroundings for a while. Several hours at Vista D'oro truly are an incredible escape. Pack a picnic or buy some snacks from the tasting room, but don't forget to stock up on wine and jam for the trip home.

Savory "Pop-Tarts"

These itty-bitty savory hand pies from Chef Lee Murphy are the perfect two-bite cocktail snack. They are a great make-ahead treat that freezes beautifully. Chef Lee recommends you make a double batch and keep a couple dozen on hand for last-minute BYOA (appies) invitations. This recipe can really be a lot of fun to play around with; try mixing and matching different herbs, cheeses, and, of course, preserves. You are limited only by your imagination!

Makes about 3 dozen pop-tarts

Pastry

2 cups all-purpose flour

½ cup finely grated parmesan + more for sprinkling

1 tsp chopped thyme leaves

½ tsp salt

½ cup cold unsalted butter

¼ cup cold vegetable shortening

2 whole eggs

¼ cup ice water

2 eggs, beaten with 2 Tbsp water for the egg wash

Filling

1 cup grated gruyère

1 jar (7.8 oz) Vista D'oro Spiced Apple and Gewürztraminer preserves

1. For the pastry, combine the flour, parmesan, thyme, and salt. Using a cheese grater, grate in the cold butter and shortening and, with your fingers, rub the mixture together to create coarse crumbs. Whisk the two whole eggs and ice water together and add to the dry ingredients. Stir just to combine. Gather into a ball, knead two to three times only, and press into a flat disk. Wrap the disk in plastic wrap and chill for at least 30 minutes.

2. Preheat the oven to 350°F. Line a baking sheet with parchment paper.

3. Roll out the chilled dough to about ⅛-inch thickness and cut it into 4- × 2-inch rectangles. Place the dough on the prepared baking sheet and brush the edges with egg wash. Place a generous pinch of grated gruyère on one end of each rectangle, top with ¼ tsp preserves, and fold the pastry in half to seal into square pouches, using a fork to press the edges together to seal tightly. Brush egg wash on top of each and sprinkle with a pinch of parmesan. Bake until golden, 25 to 30 minutes.

4. If you're making extra, fill them, pinch them, and freeze them on a sheet pan until frozen solid. Transfer them back to the freezer in a sealed plastic bag so you can take them out, thaw them, and bake them off anytime you need a fix!

Roasted Turkey Breast

Chef Lee Murphy from Vista D'oro makes creating a turkey dinner on a weeknight a breeze with this recipe! Serve with the usual sides or just a great green salad and simple roasted sweet potatoes. And yes, brining your turkey is always worth the extra effort—try it once and you'll be converted.

Serves 6

Brine
16 cups water

¼ cup kosher salt

¼ cup maple syrup

4 whole star anise

1 Tbsp whole black peppercorns

1 bay leaf

1-inch piece ginger, thinly sliced

Turkey
1 whole bone-in turkey breast (about 4 lb)

2 Tbsp unsalted butter, melted

Pepper

2 Tbsp dry white wine

2 Tbsp Vista D'oro Spiced Cranberry and Ice Wine preserves

½ cup chicken or turkey stock

Sea salt

2 Tbsp cold unsalted butter, cut in small pieces

1. For the brine, bring the water to a boil in a large saucepan. Add the salt and stir until dissolved. Add the remaining ingredients and cool to room temperature.

2. Place the turkey breast in the brine and refrigerate for 4 to 6 hours.

3. Remove the breast from the brine and dry with paper towels. Preheat the oven to 400°F.

4. Place the breast in a roasting pan, brush with melted butter, and season with pepper only. Cook for 15 minutes, then lower the oven temperature to 350°F. Roast the turkey until the internal temperature is 165°F. Baste frequently with pan juices. Remove from the oven and rest for 15 to 20 minutes.

5. Meanwhile, transfer the roasting pan with the pan drippings to the stovetop. Bring the pan juices to a boil over medium-high heat, then deglaze the pan with the wine. Add the preserves and cook for 5 minutes, stirring to incorporate. Add the stock and bring to a simmer for 10 to 15 minutes until the sauce starts to thicken and coats the back of the spoon. Season with salt and more pepper to taste. Turn off the heat and whisk in the cold butter. Slice the turkey and serve with pan sauce and extra preserves.

⇒〰

To brine a whole turkey, use the recipe above, but allow the turkey to brine for 1 hour per pound of meat. So a 12 lb turkey, for example, should soak in the brine for 12 hours. If you don't have room in your refrigerator for a giant pail of water filled with a turkey in brine, you could use an ice chest. Once you've made your brine solution, pour it into your ice chest and top it off with a 5 lb bag of ice to keep the bird cool. Close the lid and let the magic happen. When you're done, simply discard the brine solution and give your cooler a good wash.

〰⇐

Slow-Braised Beef Short Ribs

This is Chef Lee Murphy's go-to "company's coming" dinner. She can get these in the oven well before her company arrives, giving her plenty of time to clean the house and relax with a glass of wine as she waits. She suggests serving these ribs with super-decadent mashed potatoes loaded with lots of butter and fresh cream, a simple green salad tossed with a homemade balsamic vinaigrette, and, of course, lots more wine!

Serves 4

4 lb bone-in beef short ribs

Salt and pepper

2 Tbsp olive oil

1 yellow onion, chopped

3 cloves garlic, minced

Zest and juice of 1 orange

4 whole star anise

1 Tbsp whole black peppercorns, crushed

2 cups D'oro walnut wine (or your favorite port)

3 cups beef stock

½ cup Vista D'oro Figs and Walnut Wine preserves

1. Preheat the oven to 325°F.

2. Season the ribs with salt and pepper. Heat a large Dutch oven over medium-high heat. Add the oil and heat until hot but not smoking. Sear the ribs on all sides until a golden crust forms. Remove from the pan and transfer to a plate to rest.

3. To the pan, add the onions, garlic, orange zest, star anise, and peppercorns to caramelize. Deglaze the pan over medium-high heat with the wine, then add the beef stock, preserves, and orange juice and bring to a simmer, uncovered. Add the short ribs back into the liquid, stir well, and transfer the pot to the oven. Cook for 2 to 3 hours (I know it's a big time range, but it depends on the size of the ribs), until the ribs are tender and falling off the bone.

4. Transfer the ribs to a serving platter and strain the sauce into a large bowl. Put the strained sauce back into the pot and set over high heat to reduce the sauce until it coats the back of a spoon, 3 to 5 minutes. Pour the sauce over the short ribs and serve.

Milner Valley Cheese

21479 Smith Cres., Langley, V0X 1T0; 604-880-8184
milnervalleycheese.com

Goat cheese produced on the farm with milk from the farm's own herd: it really doesn't get much fresher! Located in Milner, a heritage neighborhood in the Township of Langley, Marianne and Glenn Smith run a fifth-generation heritage farm and goat dairy. The farm is pristine and the tasting room is so quaint, it makes me want to pull out a picnic!

Inside the cheeserie, you will be blown away by the selection of fresh chèvre, goat feta, cheese curds, goat jack, and colby-style cheeses. But the highlight for me is the goat gelato. Yes! Goat gelato! Made on the farm with goat milk instead of cream, this frozen treat has an incredible texture—velvety and dense—and the flavor isn't overpowered by anything sharp or "goaty." (Sometimes I find the flavor of goat milk and cheese a bit barnyard-like; it's hard to describe, but there is none of that in the gelato or in the Milner Valley cheeses.) The gelato is made with local fruit, local honey, and as many other local ingredients as they can source, so you can feel good about indulging.

Another product you should definitely try is their goat jack, made in the style of a traditional Monterey jack, a cow milk, semi-firm cheese that is usually used as a melting cheese but is often quite bland. This goat milk version of jack cheese has much more flavor—it's nutty and it has a bit of tang. Although it doesn't melt quite as well as a cow milk jack, I still like to use it the exact same way. I *love* adding this cheese to pizza, a burger, or a sandwich.

Chèvre Cheese Truffles

One of the simplest and most surprising ways to enjoy chèvre is as a truffle! There is no chocolate involved, but the combination of savory and sweet with the rich creaminess of the cheese and the crunchiness of the pistachios make this a perfect addition to a glass of BC wine!

A customer in my store told me she had enjoyed a similar dish in Spain and I was intrigued, so I created this version. I serve the truffles on small plates, tapas-style, or add them to a cheese and charcuterie board. It's fun to see the look of surprise when my guests eat their first one.

Makes about 24 truffles

1 cup shelled pistachios

8 oz fresh Milner Valley chèvre

24 seedless red or green grapes

1. To roast the nuts, preheat the oven to 350°F. Spread the pistachios on an ungreased baking sheet and roast in the oven for 8 to 10 minutes. Remove from the oven and allow to cool. In a small food processor, process the toasted pistachios until finely chopped but not powdered; set aside in a small bowl.

2. Put about 2 tsp of the chèvre in the palm of your hand, flatten it into a disk, and place a grape on top. Fold the cheese over the grape and roll it to completely cover the grape in cheese. Place it on a baking sheet. Repeat this process until all of the grapes are coated or you run out of cheese.

3. Set the baking sheet with the grapes in the refrigerator, uncovered, for about 15 minutes to firm up. Then roll the cheese-coated grapes in the chopped pistachios until coated and return them to the refrigerator until you are ready to serve them. They will keep, covered with plastic wrap, for about 4 hours, but after that the nuts lose their crunch.

4. About 15 minutes before you want to serve them, bring them to room temperature. If you want to make these ahead for a party, wait until the day you serve them to roll them in the pistachios. You can cover the grapes with cheese a day or two ahead, though.

Asparagus and Herb Chèvre Risotto

Chèvre and asparagus really should get married! They're the perfect couple.

This recipe tastes like spring to me. The rich earthiness of the asparagus pairs so well with the slightly acidic tang of the fresh chèvre. This is delicious served on its own as a main course or with a green salad. As a side dish, it can really class up a simple oven-roasted chicken. It's a recipe I've been serving variations of for years. Once you have the technique for a great risotto you can really customize the flavors to highlight seasonal ingredients like these or local mushrooms in the fall. Don't be afraid to experiment with this dish!

Serves 4

½ lb asparagus, ends trimmed

3 cups chicken or vegetable stock

4 Tbsp unsalted butter

1 Tbsp vegetable oil

½ cup finely chopped yellow onion

1½ cups Arborio rice

1 tub (6 oz) Milner Valley herb chèvre

½ cup grated parmesan

1 Tbsp chopped Italian parsley

Salt and pepper

1. Prepare a bowl of ice water.

2. In a sauté pan of salted boiling water, blanch the asparagus until the spears are fork-tender. With a set of tongs, transfer the spears to the ice water to stop the cooking immediately. Once the asparagus has cooled, cut the tips off and reserve for later. Chop the spears into ¼-inch pieces and reserve.

3. In a medium saucepan, bring the stock to a simmer over medium heat.

4. In a large heavy-bottomed sauté pan, place 2 Tbsp of the butter, the vegetable oil, and the onions and cook over medium heat until translucent. Add the rice to the saucepan. Stir to coat it well. Add a ladleful of warm stock and stir with a wooden spoon to keep the rice from sticking to the bottom of the pot. When the liquid is evaporated, add another ladleful of stock, repeating until the grains of rice lose their chalky centers and are firm yet tender, about 25 minutes.

5. Stir in the chèvre and add the asparagus stalks. When the risotto is done (it should be soft yet still slightly al dente), about another 8 minutes, turn off the heat. Stir in the remaining 2 Tbsp butter, then the asparagus tips, parmesan, and parsley. Season with salt and pepper to taste. Transfer the risotto to a serving platter and serve immediately.

Leftover risotto makes a great breakfast! Form the cold risotto into 1-inch-thick patties. Heat a nonstick frying pan over medium heat and add a bit of olive oil. Sauté the risotto cakes until golden brown and crispy. Serve them topped with an over-easy egg, a slice or two of crisp bacon, and a couple of slices of fresh tomato.

Laurica Farm

25775 – 12th Avenue, Aldergrove, V4W 2J7; 604-719-3749
Facebook: @lauricafarm

Cathy and Ian Finley came to Canada in 2009 with their two
daughters, Lauren and Jessica, from Northumberland, England.
Ian came for a job in construction—to build the roof on BC
Place Stadium in Vancouver—and they never left. They bought
their property in South Langley and really just wanted to
homestead, to live off the land and create a sustainable lifestyle
for their family. Quite quickly, Cathy found herself producing
"a little extra" and selling it or bartering with friends and
neighbors for other things she needed. Before she knew it, she

had created a Community Supported Agriculture (CSA) box and a delivery route serving about 30 local families each week. Her customers love the exceptional quality and
freshness of her produce and her pork. She claims it happened completely by accident—a lucky accident for us!

Laurica Farm (named after their girls Lauren + Jessica = Laurica) is a stunning
5-acre property just a stone's throw from the US border, right next door to Glorious
Organics. On the farm, they raise and sell pigs, chickens, sheep, and goats. There are
beautiful salad greens, eggs, and an abundance of veggies and soft fruit that grow safely
in the netted fruit cage that Ian built so they wouldn't lose half their crop to birds. But
Cathy's favorite part of the farm is the pigs. "They're funny guys," she says. She wants
people to learn that pigs are a source of more than just delicious bacon, and she loves
discussing how to use every part of the animal with her customers. When you use the
whole animal, it's actually much more economical than buying a few chops at a time.
Buying a whole pig (or cow or chicken, for that matter) that has been butchered and
packaged for you gives you quite a lot of flexibility. When you order your whole hog,
you get to decide how you want it "dressed" or prepared. You can order extra sausages,

slabs of bacon, whole smoked hams, or thick-cut pork chops. There will also be an abundance of loins, shoulders, trotters, and offal, so you'll have lots of delicious parts that you can take out of the freezer to feed your family for months to come.

Cathy takes great pride in the pigs at Laurica, and she and her girls have tons of fun naming them. At one time, the entire Kardashian family was living in the pig pen while being watched over by Big E. Smalls, a little lamb next door to the goat pen where Goaty McGoatface and Tupac were living.

Laurica Farm supplies some of the best restaurants, caterers, and chefs in the region with fresh produce and pork year-round. And kids love Laurica. There are places to run, tall grass to hide in, a giant tire swing, and a lovely miniature fairy garden to discover. The farm doesn't have a website, but you can check their Facebook page for the harvest schedule and visit the farmgate to shop or participate in one of the fabulous events hosted at the farm throughout the year, such as kids' farming camps, yoga classes, and long-table pig roasts; they have even hosted the famous Feast of Fields. There's always something happening at Laurica, so plan to visit this magical place soon. Cathy and Ian work incredibly hard, but they are gracious hosts who will always take a break to chat and share their vision for sustainable farming with you.

Scrapple

This is also known as Cathy Finley's recipe for using the "gross" bits. Organ meat is the most nutritious part of the animal, but it isn't always the most appetizing. Scrapple is delicious, but you might prefer to tell people what it's made from after they've eaten it. For me, the addition of maple syrup or homemade apple butter makes this dish, so don't leave that part out.

Serves 4 per
(9- × 5-inch) loaf

4 pig trotters

1 pork liver

1 pork heart

3 Tbsp salt

1 bay leaf

4 cups roasted cornmeal

2 tsp chopped herbs
(Cathy recommends sage
and parsley)

1 tsp pepper

1 tsp onion powder

¼ cup lard

Seasoned flour, for dusting

Maple syrup or homemade
apple butter and farm-fresh
eggs for serving

If you don't have a meat grinder or kitchen mixer with a grinding attachment, you can chop the meat very finely in a food processor, but be sure to pulse as you go. You want a very fine grind, not a paste.

1. Place the trotters and organs in a large saucepan of boiling water over high heat and cook at a rolling boil for 10 minutes. Drain and discard the water. Fill the saucepan with fresh water and bring it to a boil. Return the trotters and organs to the saucepan, and boil, uncovered, for 3 hours, checking every 30 minutes to remove any scum and topping with hot water as necessary.

2. Strain the broth into a clean saucepan and add the salt and bay leaf. Discard the trotters and put the meat through a coarse grinder. Grind the heart and liver together as finely as possible and combine the two meat mixtures.

3. Bring the broth to a simmer over medium-high heat. Combine the cornmeal, herbs, and seasonings and gradually add to the broth, stirring constantly. Turn down the heat to medium and add the ground meat mixture. Stir until everything is well mixed. Cook slowly, at a gentle simmer, for 30 minutes, stirring almost constantly so the scrapple does not stick to the bottom. It will be quite thick.

4. Use about 2 tsp of the lard to grease three 9- × 5-inch loaf pans. Pour the scrapple evenly among the three pans and set the pans aside to cool. Once cool, cover with plastic wrap and refrigerate overnight.

5. When you're ready to eat, unmold the scrapple onto a cutting board and cut it into ½-inch slices. Put the seasoned flour into a shallow dish and dredge each side of the chilled scrapple.

6. Melt the remaining lard in a skillet over medium-high heat and fry the slices until brown and crusty on both sides. Serve immediately with maple syrup or homemade apple butter alongside pasture-raised, farm-fresh eggs. The loaves will keep refrigerated in the pan, wrapped in plastic wrap, or in an airtight container for about 1 week; or they can be unmolded and frozen, wrapped tightly in aluminum foil, for up to 6 months.

Backyard Vineyards

3033 – 232nd St., Langley, V2Z 3A8; 604-539-9463
backyardvineyards.ca

Named for its proximity to Vancouver, Backyard Vineyards is "in Vancouver's backyard." As you drive north of 16th Avenue to approach the property, you can see the wrought-iron gate, the giant oak open-beam gazebo, and the winery/tasting room. It's a beautiful space surrounded by the vineyard.

In 2002, some of the nicest folks you could meet, Gary and Christina Tayler, opened Glenugie Winery. At the time, it was only the second or third winery in the Fraser Valley, and they were growing all of their own fruit and were best known for their bubbly. Sadly, in 2006, Christina passed away, and then in 2008, Gary passed. The family decided to sell the winery, and the new owners renamed it the Neck of the Woods Winery. That name didn't seem to gain a lot of traction, so it was rebranded in 2013 as Backyard Vineyards—and now they have definitely hit their stride! About 5 acres of fruit are grown on the property and are blended with fruit from the Okanagan to create award-winning reds and whites, and thankfully, they are still making fantastic bubbly.

After a visit to the tasting room, where you can enjoy a sample of everything on offer, I suggest you choose your favorite bottle, order a tasting platter of charcuterie and cheese, and, weather permitting, take it all outside to the beautiful gazebo. The giant bell inside the gazebo dates back to 1882 and was originally used to call farm workers to their meals. Now a ring of the bell is a simple request for more wine! If you happen to visit on a less-than-stellar weather day, you can enjoy your snacks and wine fireside in the tasting room. I kind of get a cozy neighborhood pub-like vibe in the tasting room, so rain or shine, you will be very comfortable at the Backyard—but beware, the time seems to pass rather quickly here. If you plan your visit ahead of time (which I recommend, because they have lots of great events, including live music and long-table dinners), you can book a tour with the winemaker, James Cambridge. He is charming, funny, and knowledgeable, of course, and has a ton of great stories to share.

Every backyard has a Nosey Neighbour, but at Backyard Vineyards, that's the name of their signature blends. Available in both red and white, they're easy drinking and well priced. However, my two current favorites at the winery are the gewürztraminer and the Blanc de Noir bubbly, but I'm a sucker for a good bubbly. The gewürztraminer is a great turkey-dinner wine, and the bubbly makes a fantastic hostess gift or a perfect local toast to any special occasion (or just because it's Friday . . .), so plan to stock up during your visit.

Backyard Vineyards' Porch is their version of a port, but they can't call it that. Just as champagne can be called champagne only if it's made in the Champagne region of France, port can be called port only if it's made in a specific way in Portugal. The fine folks at Backyard created this wine because, I suppose, they thought chocolate needed a new BFF. Not only is it perfect with chocolate, but it is also great to cook with. I've made pan sauce reductions for pork with mushrooms and cream, deglazed a frying pan full of bacon for a salad dressing, and taken their advice and enjoyed a glass of it while watching the summer sunset. Don't leave without a bottle or two!

Cranberry Sauce with Porch Wine

I'm sure you are quite familiar with the good old cranberry sauce that comes in a can—it often gets pearled out during high holidays, sometimes left as a whole blob, sliced into rounds, or smashed up into a bowl to disguise the telltale indentations from the can. Its distinctive taste is more reminiscent of the tin itself than of the actual cranberry. Like I said, I'm sure you've had it; we all have. Well, this is not that. This is about as far away from that experience as you can get. My homemade cranberry sauce is one of the easiest condiments you can make: four ingredients and 15 minutes later, you have the ideal accompaniment for your roasted turkey or duck or the perfect dollop of sweetness for a slice of homemade cheesecake. You can also use it to top a baked brie or on a sandwich—or go wild and stir it into your yogurt and granola at breakfast!

Makes about 3 cups

½ cup Backyard Porch Wine (or other port-style wine)

Zest of 1 orange

½ cup orange juice

¾ cup sugar

1 bag (1 lb) fresh or frozen cranberries

1. In a medium-size saucepan over medium-high heat, combine the Porch Wine, orange zest, and orange juice and bring to a boil. Add the sugar and stir to combine. Add the cranberries, then turn down the heat to low. Stirring constantly, allow the berries to cook and burst. They'll start to pop quickly, and if you don't turn the heat down far enough, fast enough, they'll jump like molten lava out of the pan.

2. Slowly simmer until the berries have mostly burst and the sauce is starting to thicken. Remove from the heat, set the pan aside, and allow it to cool to room temperature. The natural pectin in the berries will thicken the sauce perfectly every time.

3. Transfer the sauce to a bowl to serve or to an airtight container to refrigerate. Prepared sauce will keep in the refrigerator for up to 10 days, but it also freezes beautifully in a tightly sealed container for up to 6 months.

Trading Post Brewing

Tasting Room: #107 20120 – 64th Ave., Langley, V2Y 1M8; 604-343-2337
Taphouse and Eatery: 9143 Glover Rd., Fort Langley, V1M 0E8; 604-343-2337
tradingpostbrewing.com

Located in the center of Langley just a couple of blocks east of 200th Street, Trading Post Brewing is making great beer. Drop in to their tasting room and brewery and enjoy a flight or a pint or fill your growler, and watch the brewing team hard at work in the brewery while you do so. In addition to their own great beer, there's usually an interesting guest tap, and they frequently host cask nights, when a small cask or keg of beer is ceremoniously tapped for everyone to enjoy fresh. Cask beers are usually a little more interesting than the beers put into mainstream  production. They're also how great beer is born—a successful cask can often turn into a great beer on tap.

The actual *fort* in Fort Langley is the birthplace of BC and the original trading post in the province, hence the business name. Shortly after opening the brewery and tasting room, Trading Post Brewing founder Lance Verhoeff and his team opened the Taphouse, a pub-style eatery in Fort Langley. At the Taphouse, the experience is more about food than beer, but you can still enjoy all of their beer on tap, as well as BC wines and local cider. They use local cranberries, locally roasted coffee, and as many locally sourced ingredients as possible in their beer and the food. It's a great stop for a midday refresher or a late-day wind-down, or just to connect with friends over a pint. With a menu of stouts, English-style ales, American IPAs, and contemporary sour and barrel-aged beers, Trading Post offers plenty of reasons to break some bread (which incidentally is served warm and loaded with cheese and a side of tasty hop butter), enjoy a cold one, and share in their passion for great craft beer.

Cheesy Beer Quick Bread

This isn't the same bread as the one on the Trading Post menu, but it will surely satisfy a craving when you aren't in Langley. I have to admit that I'm not a baker—I just don't have the patience for it, generally—but this quick bread recipe of mine makes it easy to get a warm loaf on the table in under an hour. It's a great accompaniment to soups, stews, or chili, or try it the next day toasted, buttered, and spread with jalapeño jelly and a slice of Farm House cheddar (page 191). Trading Post Brewing sells their Helles Lager in six-packs at lots of local liquor stores, so it's easy to always have a can on hand when the urge strikes!

Makes 1 (8- × 4-inch) loaf

3 cups all-purpose flour

3 Tbsp sugar

1 Tbsp baking powder

1 tsp fine salt

¼ tsp cayenne pepper

1 cup grated cheddar

1 can (355 mL) 1827 Helles Lager, at room temperature

1 Tbsp melted unsalted butter

1. Preheat the oven to 375°F.

2. In a medium-size bowl, add the flour, sugar, baking powder, salt, and cayenne, and whisk to combine. Stir in the cheese, then add the beer and stir to moisten all of the dry ingredients. Don't overmix or your batter will be lumpy. Pour the batter into an 8- × 4-inch nonstick loaf pan and drizzle the melted butter on top.

3. Bake the loaf for about 40 minutes or until a toothpick inserted into the center comes out clean.

4. Remove from the oven and allow the loaf to cool in the pan for about 10 minutes. Remove the loaf from the pan and transfer to a wire rack to cool slightly.

5. Serve warm with more butter for spreading. Leftover bread can be kept wrapped tightly in plastic wrap for 2 days or frozen in an airtight bag for up to 1 month.

Smoked Onion and Beer Soup

This soup by Brian Misko (see page 94) is hearty and full of flavor, a perfect lunch after raking leaves or shoveling snow. Your neighbors will be dying for an invitation when they smell the onions smoking on your grill. Make a double batch—it freezes really well and will be a lifesaver on some random Wednesday night!

Serves 4

4 large sweet onions

2–3 Tbsp olive oil

Salt

Maple wood chips

¼ cup salted butter

2–3 Tbsp all-purpose flour

1 can (355 mL) Trading Post Helles Lager

4 cups chicken or beef stock

Pepper

Aged cheddar, grated, for garnish

1. Trim the stem end of the onions and cut into quarters toward the root end, keeping the onions intact. This will help with handling the cooked onions.

2. Place the onions on a sheet of aluminum foil; crunch up the foil around the edges to stop the onions from rolling off, but keep the tops of the onions exposed. Drizzle each onion with olive oil and sprinkle with a generous amount of salt.

3. Prepare your grill for indirect cooking on medium heat. Place a foil packet of maple wood chips under the grill grate on the hot side of the grill. Place the foil "tray" of onions on the cooler side of the grill, close the lid, and let the onions smoke for 1 to 2 hours (depending on the size of the onions), changing the smoke chip packets as they burn and turn to ash.

4. Once the onions are cooked, remove from the grill and let cool so you can handle them, then slice each quarter vertically from the root to the stem end, about three slices each.

5. In a soup pot over medium heat, melt the butter, then add the sliced smoked onions and the flour. Simmer until the onions have soaked up all of the flour, then add the beer. Stir until the beer has stopped foaming and the flour has soaked up the beer. Continue cooking the flour and beer mixture for a few minutes until the flour is absorbed completely, then add the stock. Stir well. Season to taste with salt and pepper.

6. Ladle into bowls, garnish with grated cheese, and serve with fresh bread and, of course, more beer.

Chaberton Estate Winery and the Bacchus Bistro

1064 – 216th St., Langley, V2Z 1R3; 604-530-1736
chabertonwinery.com

Chaberton Estate Winery is the oldest winery in the Fraser Valley. It was founded in 1975 as Domaine de Chaberton by Claude and Inge Violet, who brought their passion for fine food and good wine to the Fraser Valley from France. The first harvest and wine sales were in 1991, and the Violets made wine in Langley for 25 years before retiring and selling the winery to Anthony Cheng and Eugene Kwan.

Claude and Inge are widely respected as pioneers in the BC wine industry. They were very community-focused and instrumental to the evolution of a burgeoning wine culture in the region. It took them a long time to figure out what would and wouldn't grow in South Langley's microclimate, but their patience and persistence ultimately paid off with a specialty in cool-climate German varietals and the creation of their signature Bacchus blend white wine, which is still produced today.

You can almost trace the growth and evolution of the winery during the last 30 years by looking at the physical differences in the three buildings on the property: the tasting room, the Bacchus Bistro, and the winery. Architecture fans will get a kick out of comparing and contrasting the three buildings.

Chaberton has something for everyone (well, everyone over the age of 19!). The winery is very accessible with lots of parking, and combined with its warm, welcoming, old-world charm, it makes a great spot for people who might not feel comfortable in trendier places. The emphasis is more on classic than trendy, which broadens its

appeal to a mix of generations and age groups. It's the kind of place where you'll feel just as comfortable taking your grandparents as you would popping in alone for some "me time" or having lunch with friends. Kids are welcome in the tasting room, and the bistro has sparkling juice and soda for them to enjoy while you sip the good stuff!

On the topic of lunch, make a reservation if you plan on enjoying a meal at Bacchus Bistro. It is a very popular place, and rightly so. Chef Ashley makes excellent food, and the French-inspired menu features as many local ingredients as he can source. Be sure to order the chocolate mousse for dessert; it is a staple on the menu for good reason!

As at all the other wineries in the area, the tasting room staff will encourage you to buy a bottle or a glass from the tasting room and head outside to one of the many picnic tables on the property to enjoy it. Winery tours are hosted several times a day and are a great way to understand a bit of the history behind Chaberton and learn about how they have grown and evolved to serve the current market, the wines they make, where the fruit comes from, and the local microclimate. Anthony and Eugene have done a remarkable job of carrying on the Violet family tradition while turning Chaberton into a big producer in the province.

Summer Salad, Niçoise Style

This salad is a simple version of a classic French composed salad that is, for me, the perfect dinner with friends on a hot summer evening, served late on the patio with a chilled class of Domaine de Chaberton's Bacchus wine. This salad makes great use of fresh veggies that are made only slightly better with a quick blanch. All of the components can be made well ahead and composed right before you are ready to eat. This salad evokes the same feelings I get when I visit Domaine de Chaberton—it's like a mini escape to France. When I created this recipe I only had canned tuna on hand, but feel free to use freshly grilled tuna if you can get it from your fishmonger.

Serves 4

Vinaigrette
¼ cup red wine vinegar

1 Tbsp Dijon mustard

1 clove garlic, minced

2 tsp anchovy paste

¼ tsp salt

¼ tsp pepper

½ cup extra virgin olive oil

Salad
2 Tbsp salt

1½ lb nugget potatoes

1 lb green beans, ends trimmed

2 heads butter lettuce

1 pint cherry tomatoes

½ cup olives (Niçoise olives are classic, but any will work)

½ small red onion, thinly sliced

4 eggs, hard-boiled and peeled

3 cans (each 6.4 oz) tuna, packed in water

1. For the vinaigrette, in a bowl, whisk the vinegar, mustard, garlic, anchovy paste, salt, and pepper together. Slowly add the olive oil, whisking constantly until blended. Set aside or refrigerate until you're ready to use. The dressing keeps well refrigerated in an airtight container for up to 4 days.

2. For the salad, fill a large saucepan of water and add 2 Tbsp salt, then set on the stove over high heat and bring to a boil. Add the potatoes and cook until they are fork-tender, about 20 minutes. With a slotted spoon, remove the potatoes from the water and allow them to steam off in a colander in the sink. In the same pot of boiling water, cook the green beans until tender, about 5 minutes. Drain them into another colander in the sink and run cool water over them for a couple of minutes to stop them from cooking. Transfer the cooled green beans and potatoes to a clean tea towel to drain and dry.

3. Meanwhile, tear the lettuce leaves into bite-size pieces and lay them on a large platter or plate to form a base. Next, cut the tomatoes in half and sprinkle over the lettuce leaves. Cut the potatoes in halves or quarters, depending on their size, and scatter them on top of the lettuce, followed by the dried green beans, olives, and onion slices. Slice the boiled eggs into quarters and place them around the platter. Finally, drain the tuna and scoop it out of the tins in large chunks onto the plate. Drizzle the vinaigrette generously over the entire salad and serve.

Fraser Valley Cider Company

22128 – 16th Ave., Langley, V2Z 1L3; 604-308-4805
fraservalleycider.ca

Craft cider, like craft beer, varies from producer to producer. The hard cider of my youth is being replaced by something refreshingly different and hyperlocal (thank goodness). At the Fraser Valley Cider Company (FVCC), everything is made from freshly pressed apples—with no sugar added—from the 1,800 trees (and 25 varieties) grown on their 12-acre farm in South Langley.

A former chemical engineer, Rachel Bolongaro convinced her husband, Sean, to buy a farm after she had taken a cider-making class. Rachel missed the cider culture of her native England and wanted to provide people with a green space to chill out and enjoy a glass.

As you meander up the driveway to the FVCC tasting room, you feel magically transported to a totally different place. You can feel the cider culture Rachel talks about. On the lawn there are lots of picnic tables with bright red umbrellas, a badminton net, bocce balls, and clusters of big red Adirondack chairs. Truly, this is a picture-perfect setting to relax and sip cider for several hours. The tasting room staff make you feel incredibly welcome and can answer all of your burning cider questions, but I suggest starting with the tasting flight, one of the best sampling values in the Valley. For a modest fee, they'll line up their bestsellers so you can indulge before you commit to just one. I mean, you've come all this way, why not taste them all? And when you start to feel a little peckish, pop back into the tasting room and order a charcuterie platter featuring tasty bits of locally produced cheese and meat (apple cider pairs great with all kinds of food, but it especially loves grilled sausages, cheese, and roasted pork). Rachel confided there could be some "Perry cider" in their future; they have planted some Perry pear trees and hope to harvest enough to start to produce "Perry, the champagne of England." I can't wait!

Rachel's Slow-Roasted Andalusian-Style Lamb

This is a terrific Sunday supper recipe from Rachel Bolongaro. The lamb almost melts into the potatoes and vegetables as it cooks, leaving it fork-tender and incredibly flavorful. Rachel loves the ease of preparation and that she can feed a crowd from a single dish!

Serves 6-8

4 cloves garlic, crushed

2 Tbsp chopped thyme leaves

2 Tbsp salt

3¼–4 lb leg of lamb

6–8 Yukon gold potatoes, sliced into ¼-inch slices

4 bay leaves

7 Tbsp olive oil

Salt and pepper

2 lb Roma tomatoes, in ¼-inch slices

2 medium yellow onions, in ½-inch slices

2 cups Fraser Valley Cider Company House Cider (or your favorite dry cider)

1. Preheat the oven to 350°F.

2. Combine the garlic, thyme, and salt in a small bowl, then rub the mix well into the lamb.

3. Mix half the potatoes with one crushed bay leaf and 1 Tbsp of the oil. Place them in the bottom of a large roasting pan and season well with salt and pepper. Place the lamb on top of the potatoes.

4. Layer the remaining potatoes, the tomatoes, the onions, and the remaining crushed bay leaves around the lamb, seasoning each layer as you go. Drizzle everything with the remaining olive oil and pour over the cider. Cover with aluminum foil and roast for 3 to 4 hours, until the lamb is fork-tender.

5. Remove the foil and turn the heat up to 425°F for 20 to 25 minutes to crisp the lamb until dark golden. Once you're happy with the color, remove from the oven and allow it to rest for 15 minutes before breaking the lamb into large chunks and serving.

Gojoy

1110 – 264th St., Langley, V4W 2M8; 604-857-3759
gojoy.ca

Peter Breederland of Gojoy is a true Canadian agriculture pioneer: a risk taker, an innovator, and an incredibly passionate farmer. Around 2010, after many years in the hothouse veggie business, he decided to try something new—and became the first person to grow goji berries in Canada. Goji berries have been used in Chinese medicine for centuries and are one of the original superfoods, but no one had ever attempted to grow them commercially in Canada. When Peter first planted his goji crop, he didn't tell anyone what he was doing. In a market full of blueberry farmers, he wanted to grow a specialty berry that appealed to a more specific clientele.

Importing fresh gojis makes no sense—they're too sensitive to temperature changes and they don't travel long distances well. They have a similar growing season to blueberries and must be harvested by hand, but then they can be eaten fresh, frozen, dried like raisins, or juiced. Peter prefers to sell his gojis fresh, but he also sells them frozen and in a smoothie "booster." Bright red and super-shiny, fresh goji berries look like tiny teardrop ornaments about the size of your pinky nail. They pop when you bite them and are juicy and very sweet, with a slightly bitter finish. An excellent source of antioxidants, they're low in calories and loaded with fiber. No wonder they're considered "super."

At Gojoy, you can visit the farm and see the goji crop in bloom. You can pick your own gojis or join a multilingual guided tour of the farm and the greenhouse operation (see the website for more details), where they also grow the cutest baby sweet bell peppers. At their farm store, you can sample fresh gojis or a goji smoothie, buy fresh or frozen gojis, and stock up on sweet peppers for your favorite recipes. Fresh gojis are gorgeous—and tasting them fresh will be an experience you won't soon forget.

Gojoy Almond Smoothie Bowl

What is a smoothie bowl? Essentially, it's an unblended smoothie topped like an ice cream sundae. I've no idea where the idea originated, but I do know they're fun to eat and fun to make. It's also fun to show off your smoothie-bowl creations on Instagram and Pinterest (or you can show off my recipe, below). All the "cool" kids are doing it!

Makes 2 big bowls (serves 2)

Smoothie
1½ cups yogurt (see sidebar)
2 medium bananas
2 large ripe peaches, sliced
1 cup blackberries
¼ cup fresh or frozen goji berries
2 Tbsp almond butter
½ cup almond milk (see sidebar)

Toppings
(this is the fun part)
2 Tbsp granola
2 Tbsp toasted sliced almonds
¼ cup blueberries
2 Tbsp goji berries
Sliced peaches
Blackberries

1. In a blender or food processor, combine the yogurt, bananas, peaches, blackberries, goji berries, almond butter, and almond milk. Process the mixture until it is completely smooth. It will be quite thick.

2. Pour that mixture into two cereal bowls and top with your favorite toppings. Photograph your creation, post it to social media, and enjoy!

───※───

Fresh goji berries are available for only a few months in the summer, so you really should make the most of them when you can get them. Fresh berries don't store well, so you'll need to eat them within a couple of days of buying them, or you can freeze them like so: After washing the berries, air-dry them on a clean towel and then lay them out in a single layer on a sheet pan. Pop the whole pan into the freezer until the berries are frozen solid, then transfer the frozen berries to a freezer storage bag and put them back into the freezer for safekeeping. Now you'll have delicious local goji berries on hand to make your smoothie bowl sexy all year long! (This freezing method works great for all of your summer berries.)

The yogurt from Farm House Natural Cheeses (page 191), is *amazing* and will totally elevate your smoothie-bowl experience. Regular milk also works for this recipe, but I like the extra nuttiness that almond milk adds.

───※───

Glorious Organics Co-op

1374 – 256th St., Langley, V4W 2J4; 604-857-1400
gloriousorganics.com

Glorious Organics is a certified organic, co-operatively owned business that operates on Fraser Common Farm in South Langley. I met Susan Davidson, the founder of Glorious Organics, in 2007, and I was instantly taken by her quick wit and her commonsensical, grassroots, passionate, and charming personality. Susan has been farming in Langley since 1980; she raised her kids on the farm, and now her grand-children enjoy the farm life.

In 2007, Susan and I, along with a group of like-minded individuals, worked on creating a farmers market in Langley. Led by Gary Jones, a sustainable horticulture professor at Kwantlen Polytechnic University in Langley, we coughed and sputtered, made mistakes, and learned many lessons, but eventually opened the Langley Community Farmers Market in May 2009. The market is still running today, with a new board of directors and new leaders at the helm to keep it flourishing. In the 7 to 8 years that I worked with Susan, I came to have incredibly deep respect and admiration for her, for her passion for sustainable agriculture and the earth, and for her need to educate and share information about why food security is so incredibly important and why we should all take it more seriously. Susan stands up for what she believes in—she isn't afraid to speak her mind and obviously isn't afraid to get her hands dirty. She's my kind of girl!

Susan has always been best known for her greens and edible plant garnishes—her boutique lettuces, salad mixes, and microgreens are some of the best in the world—but the farm has grown and evolved over the years, and it now supplies home cooks and some of the best chefs in the country with all kinds of organic produce. Twelve staff work on the farm, growing an assortment of produce, herbs, and some fruit, and they have a small flock of hens for egg production. Fraser Common Farm doesn't have a regular farmgate, but you can find Glorious Organics at a few of the local farm markets, and on their website you can sign up for a Community Supported Agriculture (CSA) box or check their fresh sheet for seasonal offerings and where to find them.

The farm also hosts a couple of events each year and has become especially well known for an annual dinner called Forage, a joint effort with local breweries, cheeseries, wineries, and other farms. Chef Chris Whittaker, the owner of Forage restaurant in Vancouver, comes out to Fraser Common to prepare an amazing long-table supper, usually featuring a whole roasted pig. The date is announced early, and if you're interested in attending, you should look at the website now to book your tickets, as it sells out quickly. In addition to the Forage event, the farm hosts a summer farm camp for kids and workshops on a wide array of topics, all in an effort to educate the next generation, to get kids connected to the land and to their food. Susan Davidson and everyone at Fraser Common Farm are leaving quite a legacy in our community.

Quick Pickled Cucamelons

One of the most interesting things I've ever purchased from Glorious Organics at a farm market has to be their cucamelons. They might just be the cutest vegetable ever grown. They look like tiny green watermelons, about the size of a grape, but taste like a slightly tart cucumber on the inside. Cucamelons are super-adorable cut in half and used as a garnish on a salad—that is, if the bag makes it home from the market. I've given you my pickle recipe here, but you can also use cucamelons in salsa. Try this pickle as an interesting garnish in a martini or Caesar (or Bloody Mary, of course) or on a seasonal cheese and charcuterie board.

Makes 4 cups

1½ cups white vinegar

¼ cup sugar

1 tsp coarse salt

1 clove garlic, sliced

2 Tbsp chopped dill

1 Tbsp chopped mint

1 tsp coriander seeds

1 tsp yellow mustard seeds

1½ cups cucamelons

1. In a medium-size saucepan over medium-high heat, bring the vinegar to a boil, then add the sugar and salt and whisk until completely dissolved. Remove from heat, add the garlic slices, and allow to cool completely.

2. Stir in the dill, mint, and coriander and mustard seeds.

3. Wash the cucamelons and put them in a sterile jar (see sidebar; a 4-cup canning jar with a tight-fitting lid works best). Pour the seasoned vinegar into the jar over the cucamelons and seal tightly.

4. Refrigerate for at least a week, or 2 weeks if you can wait that long. They will keep for up to 4 months in a sealed jar.

⋙

To sterilize your jar and lid, simply place them in a saucepan of boiling water and let them simmer for 15 minutes. Remove from the water with tongs and place inverted onto a wire rack to cool and dry. When you can handle the jar, turn it over and fill as desired.

⋘

JD Farms

24726 – 52nd Ave., Langley, V2Z 1E2; 604-856-2431
jdfarms.ca

It doesn't matter the time of day, the day of the week, or the season—when you open the front door and walk into the farm store at JD Farms, you can smell turkey roasting, pie baking, and coffee brewing. JD Farms feels like home, and the Froese family makes everyone feel so welcome.

Jack and Debbie Froese have been farming on 248th Street (yes, I know their address is 52nd Ave., but they're on the corner of 248th and 52nd, and the powers that be made 52nd the address) in Langley since 1979. They raise turkey, lots and lots of turkey. Well, actually, they also raised three pretty great kids, who now have kids of their own and can all be found at the farm or working in the bistro at some point during the week. JD Farms is a true family business.

JD turkeys are raised in the large barns you can see as you go up the driveway to the farmgate, where the turkeys have tons of space to roam and plenty of access to fresh water and nonstop feed. You can buy fresh and frozen whole birds, turkey pieces—both cooked and raw—and a massive assortment of turkey products like pot pies, lasagna, soup, chili, meatballs, and sausages, all made fresh with JD Farms' specialty turkey meat and using their own signature recipes. One of my favorite things about a visit to JD Farms is that there's always that "one guy" walking around with a smoked turkey drumstick in his hand and a giant smile on his face. My other favorite thing is a cold turkey sandwich, made just the way I like it—dark meat on cranberry sourdough with lots of mayo, cranberry sauce, lettuce, and a slice of cheddar. The staff are happy to make your sandwich—

however you prefer it—to order. You can eat your lunch inside the bistro or enjoy the sunshine on the patio.

On a more serious note, turkeys don't cost $0.79 per pound. Cheap birds are used as loss leaders during holidays, meant to draw discount shoppers to chain stores, where they pay too much for other things. It creates a false economy, and I know you, a savvy local shopper, won't be fooled by these kinds of tactics. You want a bird you know has had a healthy life, has been fed good feed and slaughtered humanely, and puts food on the table of lots of local farmers, their families, and their staff. I think it's important that we make those connections with our food every day.

The last question you need to ask as you pull out of the JD Farms driveway onto 248th Street with a belly full of turkey is: Do I turn right or do I turn left? Krause Berry Farms is 3 minutes due north. Bonetti Meats is 2 minutes due south. Decisions, decisions.

Turkey Picadillo

This is my version of picadillo, a great Cuban dish traditionally made with ground beef, but ground turkey is a great alternative. The sweetness of the raisins and the briny saltiness of the olives with the crunchy toasted almonds is such a great combination with the rich turkey meat. You can eat picadillo like a chili or with a bit of steamed basmati rice, but it's also perfectly delicious sprinkled with some grated cheese and rolled inside a soft tortilla. And like most stews or chilies, it always tastes better the next day—so why not make a double batch?

Serves 4

2 Tbsp olive oil

1 lb ground turkey thigh meat

2 cloves garlic, chopped

1 medium yellow onion, diced

1 Tbsp tomato paste

2 medium field tomatoes, roughly chopped

2 tsp chili powder

1 tsp salt

½ tsp ground cinnamon

½ tsp ground cumin

¼ tsp ground cloves

⅛ tsp red pepper flakes

1 medium red bell pepper, diced

⅓ cup golden raisins

½ cup chicken or turkey stock

¼ cup sliced pimento-stuffed olives

¼ cup toasted slivered almonds

Pepper

1 small handful cilantro, chopped, for garnish

1. In a 10-inch frying pan over medium-high heat, heat the olive oil and brown the turkey, breaking it up with a wooden spoon while it cooks. Add the garlic and onions and sauté until fragrant but not browned. Add the tomato paste, tomatoes, chili powder, salt, cinnamon, cumin, cloves, and red pepper flakes. Stir to combine. Add the bell peppers and the raisins. Stir to combine.

2. Add the stock and let all of the ingredients cook together, stirring occasionally, until the turkey is fully cooked and the bell peppers are tender, about 5 minutes. Turn down the heat to medium-low, stir in the olives and finally the almonds just to warm through, then taste for seasoning and adjust as required with salt and pepper.

3. Remove from the heat and serve sprinkled with chopped cilantro.

Leftover Turkey Tortilla Soup

This soup is a recipe I created as a way to repurpose turkey leftovers. If you like things spicier, add more chili powder or some cayenne, or garnish it with more freshly sliced jalapeños. For a milder version, leave the jalapeños out entirely.

Serves 2

3 Tbsp olive oil

1 small yellow onion, finely chopped

2 Tbsp chili powder

4 cups homemade turkey or chicken stock

1 can (28 oz) stewed diced tomatoes

1 can (14 oz) white kidney beans, drained and rinsed

2 cups diced cooked turkey (leftovers are perfect)

1 cup fresh or thawed frozen corn

1 cup coarsely broken corn tortilla chips

2 tsp minced jalapeños, stems, seeds, and ribs removed

Salt and pepper

Hot sauce (optional)

1 avocado, diced, for garnish

4 Tbsp grated aged cheddar or mozzarella, for garnish

¼ cup chopped cilantro, for garnish

1 lime, in wedges, for garnish

1. Place the olive oil in a heavy, medium-size saucepan over medium heat, then add the onions and chili powder. Stir constantly just until fragrant and the onions start to sweat, about 3 minutes.

2. Add the stock and stewed tomatoes with their juices. Increase the heat to medium-high and bring to a boil. Add the beans, turkey, corn, ⅓ cup of the tortilla chips, and the minced jalapeños.

3. Simmer, uncovered, until the vegetables are tender, about 10 minutes. Season the soup to taste with salt and pepper and your favorite hot sauce if you like a bit more heat.

4. Ladle the soup into deep bowls, dividing equally. Sprinkle with the remaining tortilla chips, top with some diced avocado, grated cheese, and cilantro, and serve with a fresh lime wedge for squeezing.

5. This soup freezes really well. Just reheat and garnish when you are ready to serve.

Bonetti Meats

3986 – 248th St., Langley, V4W 2B3; 604-856-2187
bonettimeats.com

When Italo and Jackie Bonetti founded Bonetti Meats in 1973, I'm sure they had no idea that 40 years later, a third generation of butchers would be rolling up their sleeves and learning the craft from their father. Carlo Bonetti bought the shop from his parents several years ago and is now teaching his sons, Enzo and Michael, the traditional family recipes he learned from his dad, Italo. I can't even tell you how happy it makes me to pull up to the shop and see one of the boys coming out of the smokehouse with a giant grin on his face, thrilled with the way the product they're making is coming along. Carlo always has a minute to stop and say hello and to ask what I'm cooking. You feel like part of the family at Bonetti Meats, and the pride they take in their work is evident in all of their products. Butchery is a skill—dare I say, a dying art—that we need to encourage and support, and the best way to do that is to get to know your butcher on a first-name basis! At the chain grocery stores, you'll find product that has come in on pallets in boxes from big production facilities in far-off places. The meat is placed on a Styrofoam tray wrapped in plastic, and you have no idea how long it has been there or where it came from. At Bonetti Meats, they weigh everything to order and wrap it in old-fashioned butcher's paper. Extra care and attention are taken by everyone, every step of the way, and it shows.

Bonetti Meats is everything you think of when you think about an old-school butcher shop. Carlo and his team bring in whole animals from local farms and producers and break them down on site, making it possible for you to get any cut you want anytime you want. If you don't see what you want in the case, just ask. Someone will go to "the back" and have one of the butchers cut it for you. This is what I love

about shopping at Bonetti Meats. They can tell you exactly where the meat came from, usually the first name of the person who raised it, how long it has been aged, or tips and tricks for the best way to cook it. They also have a fantastic assortment of house-made sausages made the old-fashioned way with high-quality meat, spices, and seasonings, as opposed to mystery meat, preservatives, and fillers. And the product from the smokehouse is incredible. They easily make the very best ham in the Fraser Valley, and their Appetizer Sausage is a bit reminiscent of a garlic sausage, only smokier and seriously addictive—and made only slightly better when accompanied by a chunk of cheddar and a glass of wine. Bratwurst, pepperoni, bacon, smokies, and even hot dogs are made on site. Bonetti hot dogs are a must-have for campfires and trips to the lake. They're made fresh, and you can identify every single ingredient. The kids are going to love them. Make sure you pack a cooler with an ice pack when you visit—you're definitely going to want to stock up!

Bonetti's Sweet Italian Sausage with Caramelized Onions and Apples

Bonetti Meats is just a few doors down from Annie's Orchard (page 74), making this recipe a natural choice. Carlo Bonetti will tell you that in Italy, they would traditionally serve their sausage on buns with a mixture of sautéed sweet peppers and onions, but when I first created this dish, I didn't have any peppers on hand so I improvised, and I think the addition of apples to the recipe is really a cool twist. I do have to say that the mustard you choose for this recipe is important. Use one you really love and be generous with it. It contrasts perfectly with the apples and the richness of the sausage.

Serves 4

1 Tbsp olive oil

1 medium onion, thinly sliced

2 large Bramley apples, thinly sliced into thin wedges

1 Tbsp apple cider vinegar

1 Tbsp brown sugar

Salt and pepper

4 sweet Italian-style sausages

4 soft sausage buns

4 Tbsp grainy mustard

1. Preheat your BBQ to medium-high heat (about 375°F).

2. In a frying pan over medium-high heat, add the oil and the onions and cook until the onions are translucent but not starting to brown. Add the apples, vinegar, and brown sugar and cook, stirring occasionally, until the mixture is soft and starts to caramelize, about 10 minutes. Turn down the heat to medium-low and season to taste with salt and pepper.

3. Meanwhile, grill the sausages, turning them occasionally, until they're golden brown and cooked through, about 12 minutes. Remove from the grill and add them to the sauté pan with the onion and apple mixture, still over medium-low heat. Allow the sausages to rest on top of the onion and apple mixture while you prepare the buns.

4. Cut the buns open and generously spread them with the grainy mustard. (You can also toast the buns first, if you like.) Add one sausage to each bun and pile high with the caramelized apples and onions. Serve immediately.

If you don't have a BBQ, you can fry the sausages in a separate pan over medium heat until golden and cooked through or place them in an ovenproof dish and set them under the broiler.

Annie's Orchard

4092 – 248th Street, Aldergrove, V4W 1E3; 604-856-3041

An apple a day! At least from mid-August through the end of October. At Annie's Orchard (conveniently located halfway between JD Farms [page 65] and Bonetti Meats [page 70] to add a little fruit and fiber to your carnivorous shopping spree), you'll find about 60 varieties of apples. SIXTY.

Jim and Mary Ann Rahe started selling apples on their 7-acre farm in 1983. They have about 5 acres of orchard with about 3,000 trees producing fruit. The apples ripen at different times, so there's always something coming out of the orchard, but Jim says the Gravensteins are the most popular.

Apples = comfort food. There's nothing like an apple crisp fresh from the oven, an apple pie cooling on the pie rack, or applesauce simmering on the stove—all sure signs of fall. They all come with the warm aromas of cinnamon, cloves, butter, and toasting oats. It makes my insides warm just thinking about it!

Both heritage and regional varieties are available at different harvest times during the season, everything from the Bramley, the classic apple crumble apple, to the Gravenstein, the perfect applesauce apple! Northern Spy apples are ideal for baking and storing, and kept in a cool, dark place, they'll last for months. The Cox's Orange Pippin is not necessarily the best apple for cooking, but should be enjoyed freshly picked from the tree, wiped on your pant leg, and eaten immediately with the juices running down your arm. Conversely, the Belle de Boskoop, a greenish-yellow apple with rough skin, perfectly crisp and tangy, only tastes better when you store it for several months before eating it. Chefs love Belle de Boskoops for their ability to hold up in the oven.

So many apples, so little time. Oh, and there are 12 varieties of pears—good luck deciding which of those you want to try first!

Easy Slow-Cooker Applesauce

This is one of my favorite fall recipes. Very little effort and a flip of the switch on the old slow cooker make this a recipe you're going to be glad you took the time to make. You can serve my sauce alongside roasted pork, add it to your morning granola, or just eat it straight out of the refrigerator. The kids will love it in their lunches, and you can bake with it or mash it into roasted turnips. (Or try it in Mom Taves's Applecake, page 133.) PS: Your house is going to smell amazing!

Makes 5 cups

4 lb Gravenstein apples, peeled and thinly sliced (about 12 cups)

½ cup sugar

1 tsp ground cinnamon

1 cup apple juice or cider (not from concentrate)

1 Tbsp lemon juice

1. Place the apples in a slow cooker, sprinkle with the sugar and cinnamon, and stir to combine. Pour over the apple juice (or cider) and lemon juice and stir again. Cook on low for about 6 hours or on high for 3 hours. The apples will cook down. Stir them occasionally to break them up.

2. When you are satisfied with the saucy consistency, allow the sauce to cool, then transfer to airtight containers to freeze for up to 4 months or refrigerate for up to 2 weeks.

Krause Berry Farms

6179 – 248th St., Langley, V4W 1C3; 604-856-5757
krauseberryfarms.com

If Walt Disney had been a berry farmer, I think he would have created Krause Berry Farms, a magical kingdom where you can find *everything* berry! In 1974, Alf Krause planted 1 acre of strawberries. He could have had no idea at that time that he and his wife, Sandee, would eventually build what is today essentially a theme park on a working farm, dedicated to fresh strawberries, blueberries, raspberries, and blackberries. On their more than 200 acres, they grow berries and an assortment of veggies: nugget potatoes, sweet corn, and green beans. As you drive up to the farmgate, you'll see the strawberry fields and the blueberry-colored buildings. You'll feel the anticipation in your car grow and your passengers perk up as you see the signs pointing to the winery, the bakery, the fudgery, and the Porch café. (The bakery, fudgery, and café are all in one delicious building.)

Sandee is the baker in the family. Recipes that have been passed down to her combine with recipes she's created to fill the shelves in the market with more than 100 different products—fresh bread, jams, jellies, fruit-filled perogies, fresh berry ice cream, scones, and pies . . . OH MY, THE PIES! The fresh berry custard pie towers over everything else in the case like the crown jewel of desserts. On the patio at the Porch café, you can enjoy lunch offerings such as a roasted corn pizza made with fresh Krause sweet corn, or a "krausedilla" filled with melted cheese and served with fresh-cut salsa; or if you're there in time for breakfast, try a giant waffle piled high with berries (of course) and a massive cloud of whipped cream.

Take time to visit the winery, too. Pull up a saddle stool and taste some of their table wines made from apples, rhubarb, and every berry on the farm, or a port-style wine made from blackberries and currants. Or you can turn your visit to the farm into a real celebration while enjoying a glass of their award-winning raspberry sparkling wine, a perfect summer sipper, on the patio with a friend and a slice or two of pie or a bit of something rich and chocolaty.

But Krause Berry Farms isn't just about eating and drinking! There's so much to see and do, it's hard to decide where to start. You can pick your own berries (BYO container), take a tractor-train ride, or participate in a myriad of fantastic events like the Annual Butterfly Release. Check their website for a list of activities and the timing of the berry harvest so you can be sure to make the most of your visit.

The Krause family motto has always been, "Be good to the land and the land will be good to you." They are obviously very good to the land, because their land rewards them, year after year, with an incredible bounty of luscious berries. The berry business is hard work, and farm management is something Alf Krause is passionate about. From using ultramodern techniques to manage pests and taking every step possible to avoid treating their crops with pesticides, Alf and his team work hard to give their customers some of the best-quality berries that can be grown in the region, and it is obvious in the flavor of the fruit. After decades as berry farmers, Sandee and Alf still love what they do and are great ambassadors for agritourism in Canada.

Raspberry and Herb Nugget Potato Salad

This is not your grandmother's potato salad. The first time I added raspberries to this salad it was an accident. I was multi-tasking in the kitchen and apparently got a little carried away but the result was so great, I have made it a bunch of times since. The yogurt and tartness of the fresh raspberries make it zippy and less cloyingly creamy than a mayo-based salad. Feel free to change up the berries and herbs if raspberries aren't available. Try blueberries and flat-leaf parsley with red wine vinegar or blackberries and cilantro with champagne vinegar.

Serves 4

2 lb local nugget potatoes

4 Tbsp Krause Berry Farms raspberry vinegar

1 cup Greek-style plain 2% yogurt

¼ cup chopped flat-leaf parsley

1 Tbsp finely chopped tarragon

1 red bell pepper, thinly sliced

⅓ cup thinly sliced celery

½ cup raspberries

Salt and pepper

¼ cup finely chopped green onions or chives

1. In a large saucepan of salted, boiling water, cook the potatoes until they are fork-tender, about 20 minutes. Drain well and return to the saucepan. Stir them with a large wooden spoon, breaking some of the potatoes up while drizzling with about half of the raspberry vinegar. Allow the potatoes to steam off and absorb the vinegar, about 5 minutes. Transfer them to a large bowl and allow them to cool completely.

2. Meanwhile, prepare the dressing. In a small bowl, whisk together the yogurt, the remaining vinegar, and the parsley and tarragon.

3. Add the bell peppers, celery, and dressing to the cooled potatoes, and toss to combine. Fold in the fresh berries and season to taste with salt and pepper. Sprinkle over the green onions (or chives) and serve.

Fresh Strawberry Basil Lemonade

This tastes like summer in a glass! Made from berries at the peak of ripeness and super-fragrant fresh basil, this is my recipe for the perfect summer sipper! I probably don't need to tell you how fabulous this can be with the addition of your favorite local gin or vodka. Cheers!

Makes about 3 (2-cup) servings

2 cups sliced strawberries

1 cup + 2 Tbsp sugar

3 cups filtered water

Zest of 3 lemons

½ cup tightly packed basil

1½ cups lemon juice (about 8 lemons)

More basil and berries, for garnish

1. Put the strawberries in a bowl, sprinkle with 2 Tbsp of the sugar, and set aside to rest at room temperature.

2. In a small saucepan over high heat, boil the water, then add the remaining 1 cup sugar and the lemon zest. Stir until the sugar dissolves. Remove from the heat and add the basil leaves. Congratulations. You've just made a simple syrup.

3. Cover with a lid and let steep at room temperature for about 10 minutes. Strain through a fine-mesh sieve into a large pitcher and allow to cool to room temperature. Discard the basil leaves.

4. To the pitcher, add the sweetened berries and lemon juice. Top with fresh, cool water. Stir well to combine. Transfer to the refrigerator to chill. When you're ready to serve, fill your glasses with ice and top with lemonade. Garnish with a sprig of fresh basil and a whole fresh berry.

Leaving the hulls on strawberries keeps them fresh longer.
Hull them right before you are going to eat them.

Bird's Nest Cookies

This recipe comes from Sandee Krause. It is an incredibly meaningful recipe to her. Her father's mother, Sarah Greene, made these cookies for her family and filled them with her homemade jam. Sandee has continued making them for her six children and now for her three grandchildren. At the farm, you can find them in the pastry case at Christmas. Sandee loves sharing them with visitors to the Krause Berry Farms bakery.

Makes about 3 dozen cookies

1 cup salted butter

1 cup vegetable shortening, at room temperature

1 cup brown sugar

4 whole eggs, separated

1 tsp pure vanilla extract

4 cups all-purpose flour

1 tsp salt

1 cup quick oats

1 jar Krause Berry Farms raspberry or blueberry jam

1. Preheat the oven to 350°F. Line a baking sheet with parchment paper.

2. In a large bowl, using an electric mixer, beat the butter, shortening, brown sugar, egg yolks, and vanilla until smooth. Add the flour and salt and mix on low speed until completely blended.

3. In a separate bowl, beat the egg whites until slightly foamy. Set aside.

4. Put the quick oats in a small bowl and set aside.

5. With an ice cream scoop, remove a scoop of dough from the bowl and roll it into a 2-inch ball. Place it on the prepared baking sheet. Continue until all the dough has been formed into balls. Dip each dough ball into the egg whites, then roll in the quick oats.

6. Place the oat-coated dough balls back on the prepared baking sheet. Use the handle of a wooden spoon to make a small indent in the center of each cookie ball. Bake until golden brown, 15 to 18 minutes. Remove from the oven and allow them to cool. Fill the indentation with the jam, and serve.

7. These cookies freeze well. Freeze them as raw dough balls after you roll them in oats. When the craving strikes, thaw them, make the indentation, and bake them, then fill with your favorite jam right before you serve them. The cookies can be frozen after you've baked them and added the jam, but they'll stick together, so it's best to fill them right before you're going to enjoy them.

Driediger Farms

23823 – 72nd Ave., Langley, V1M 3K9; 604-888-1665
driedigerfarms.com

As you arrive at Driediger Farms on a warm summer morning, you can actually smell the berries when you open your car door. It's incredible! Rhonda Driediger is a second-generation Langley farmer who grows strawberries, raspberries, blackberries, red currants, and blueberries on 160 acres. That's a lot of berries. Much of what is grown here is picked, packed, and shipped fresh all over Canada and the world. Driediger is one of the biggest exporters of berries in BC, but there's always plenty for local customers to enjoy.

Rhonda took over the family farm from her parents, June and George, who started farming in Langley in the 1960s. She takes the business of fresh berries super-seriously and is a dedicated advocate for quality farming practices in the berry industry. From May through September, you can find some of the best berries in the Valley right here.

Driediger Farms is on 72nd Avenue, which is literally the road to berry heaven. The single-lane road meanders past many other commercial blueberry farms, roadside stands, and honor boxes selling berries, fresh flowers, and sometimes local honey. As you crest the hill at 237th Street, you'll see a ton of colorful little dots all over the berry fields. It always takes a minute to register that all of those dots are actually the hats of customers picking fresh berries in the Driediger fields. As you approach, drive slowly—families will be crossing the road from the U-pick fields with their full buckets to the farm market, where they'll weigh and pay for their harvest. If you plan to try the U-pick, aim to arrive early in the day—berries like cooler temperatures, so it's best to pick in the morning if you can. Bring a container with a handle—an ice cream pail works well—and sunscreen and a hat. But don't bring your dog. Dogs aren't allowed in the U-pick fields, and the last thing you want to do is leave your furry friend in a hot car while you pick berries. So please, leave your dog at home.

If you don't want to U-pick, you can shop at the market and easily get your fill to eat now or to freeze or preserve for later. There's plenty of parking at the farm and the signage is good.

Rhonda plants six varieties of strawberries to ensure there's always something delicious coming off the field. Typically, strawberries are available in May, June, August, and September, but check the harvest schedule on their website before you head out so you can be sure to get exactly what you want!

You can usually spot a berry picker from 20 paces by the color of their hands. For some it's a badge of honor, the price you must pay for berry deliciousness, because let's face it, wearing rubber gloves to pick or process berries is no fun at all. To remove berry stains from your hands, soak them in a bowl of hot water with dish soap and a good squeeze of fresh lemon juice. Shake off the excess water and rub ½ tsp salt between your damp hands before rinsing them. The abrasiveness of the salt should remove any residual staining.

Family Favorite Strawberry Shortcake

One of the best ways to enjoy any of the fresh Driediger berries is in a simple shortcake. This is June Driediger's family recipe. If anyone knows their way around a strawberry shortcake, I think it's June! The thing I appreciate about this recipe is that it's more cakey than scone-like. Both are good, but this one is a real treat!

Serves 6

Shortcake
½ cup unsalted butter

1 cup sugar

2 eggs

1½ cups cake and pastry flour

2 tsp baking powder

Pinch of fine salt

¾ cup whole milk

Topping
Sugar to taste

2 cups sliced strawberries

Vanilla ice cream, for serving

Whipped cream, for serving

1. Preheat the oven to 350°F. Butter and flour an 8-inch square cake pan.

2. For the shortcake, in a medium-size bowl, use an electric mixer to cream the butter with the sugar. Add the eggs one at a time and mix to combine. In a separate bowl, sift together the flour, baking powder, and salt.

3. With the mixer on low, add half the milk and half the flour mixture to the butter mixture until well combined. Add the other half of both, and mix to combine.

4. Pour the batter into the prepared cake pan and bake for 20 minutes, or until a toothpick inserted in the center comes out clean. Remove from the oven and transfer to a wire rack to cool.

5. For the topping, while your cake cools, sprinkle sugar over the berries and stir gently to coat, then allow them to sit, uncovered, at room temperature for at least 5 minutes, or up to 30 minutes. The amount of sugar you use will depend on the ripeness and sweetness of the berries and your personal taste; start with 1 Tbsp sugar, let the berries sit for 5 minutes, and taste them again. Continue to adjust the sweetness as necessary.

6. Cut the shortcake into six pieces, slice them in half horizontally, and fill with ice cream. Top the filled squares with the sweetened berries and a generous dollop of whipped cream. Serve immediately. Store leftover shortcake and berries separately, and assemble them just before you serve them. The shortcake will store well in the refrigerator, in an airtight container for 2 to 3 days, but the prepared berries should be eaten within a day.

Strawberry Freezer Jam

The first time I had freezer jam, it was a recipe my mom made. I was so blown away by the intense flavor of the spreadable strawberries that I made my own simple recipe and have been using it ever since. This jam will allow you to enjoy the flavors of freshly picked local strawberries all year! If you've never had or made freezer jam, you're going to want to add this to your repertoire at your first opportunity. Freezer jam can be made in a snap, and it's great on toast, over ice cream, stirred into yogurt, blended into a shake, or just eaten straight from the spoon. Oh, and it tastes just like summer!

Makes about 3 cups

4 cups sugar

2 cups chopped ripe strawberries

1 package (1¾ oz) dry pectin

¾ cup water

1. In a medium-size bowl, pour the sugar over the berries and gently mix to combine. Let them stand for 10 minutes to release some of their natural juices, then use a potato masher to gently crush the berries into a chunky, jammy consistency.

2. While your berries are sitting, in a small saucepan over medium-high heat, stir the pectin into the water and bring it to a boil for 1 minute, then pour it over the crushed berries. Stir to combine and allow to stand for 3 minutes to start to thicken, then stir again and pour the mixture into clean freezer-safe containers, being careful to leave about an inch of space at the top to allow for expansion during freezing.

3. Cover the containers with tight-fitting lids and let them sit at room temperature for 24 hours. Transfer the containers to the freezer for up to a year and thaw when you need them. Once thawed, a jar of jam will last for 3 to 4 weeks in the refrigerator. (At my house, we use clean single-serve yogurt containers with plastic lids. They hold the perfect amount of jam for a weekend, and it's a great way to reuse the packaging—plus, we're fancy like that.)

The Fort Wine Co. Estate Winery

26151 – 84th Ave., Langley, V1M 3M6; 604-857-1101
thefortwineco.com

You know that juice commercial where the father and son are standing in a cranberry bog and talking about not adding sugar to their juice? It could have easily been filmed in Fort Langley. Langley is one of the biggest suppliers of cranberries in Canada. If you happen to find yourself in Langley on the Saturday of the Thanksgiving weekend, you must visit the Fort Langley Cranberry Festival and tour a working cranberry bog. As an added bonus, you can do it while sipping a glass of wine from one of BC's most prolific fruit wineries, the Fort Wine Co.

Founded in 2001 by tugboat captain and cranberry farmer Wade Bauck, the winery now produces 11 different kinds of wine and, in doing that, supports many local berry and fruit farms. The cranberries come from right there behind the tasting room, though—each year's harvest from 8½ acres of cranberry bog turn into Fort Wine Co.'s flagship Mighty Fraser cranberry table wine and their Saucy cranberry fortified wine.

The drive from Fort Langley or Highway 1 to the Fort Wine Co. can be quite distracting. The scenery is breathtaking, and just as you start to question your ability to navigate and think you might have passed it, it appears like an oasis at the end of a long gravel driveway. A quaint cottage-type building, set against a background of cranberry fields and the Mighty Fraser River (locals always capitalize "Mighty," even in conversation), provides an incredibly warm welcome and serves as a tasting room and bistro. Right beside the tasting room is the patio, which is a hive of activity from early spring to late fall. The water dish on the ground beside the patio is a reminder to keep your four-legged friends hydrated on a hot day and lets you know they're welcome to take a walk and stretch their legs—on a leash, of course. Inside the tasting room, you can—you guessed it—taste. There's something for just about everyone. Table wines are simple and fresh-tasting; some are dry and tart, while others are great mix-ins for your favorite sangria recipe. The fortified wines, similar to an ice wine, are nothing short of spectacular. Their flavors are intensely concentrated and fresh—only the highest-quality fruit could result in a finished product that tastes that good! A splash of their fortified wine in a martini is a total game changer, and their Isle Queen blackberry port-style wine might just be one of the greatest ways ever bottled to finish a cheese course.

About 50 percent of BC's cranberry crop is used to make sweetened dried cranberries, 40 percent is made into juice, 9 percent is sold whole frozen, and 1 percent is sold fresh, according to the Government of BC.

In the late 1800s, cranberries were a hot trading commodity at Fort Langley. First Nations peoples used them for food, dyes, and medicine. They would trade cranberries for Hudson's Bay Company blankets and beads. In 1858, cranberries were actually worth more than salmon.

On the patio, you can enjoy a bottle purchased in the tasting room along with a cheese plate composed of local cheese, charcuterie, and preserves, or you can simply sit and sip in the shade of the wine garden, chat with friends, take your shoes off, and enjoy the scenery.

Finger Fruit Ice Cream

Finger Fruit is what the Fort Wine Co. calls their fortified raspberry wine. A single sip is like eating the most luscious, perfectly ripe raspberry you have ever had on the most perfect summer day. Your first taste is truly unforgettable. You can relive the flavors of summer all year long just by taking out your corkscrew.

I use my countertop electric ice cream maker all summer. This is my go-to vanilla ice cream base with the addition of the fortified wine. It's super simple and screams summer! Serve it with fresh fruit—I love it with super-ripe peaches—or eat it on your patio straight out of the ice cream maker and drizzled with chocolate sauce. It's best when shared with friends, but be warned, you're going to need to make another batch almost immediately, so get that ice cream tub back in the freezer!

Serves 4

4½ cups whipping cream

1 cup sugar

Pinch of salt

¾ cup Fort Wine Co. Finger Fruit fortified raspberry wine (or other fortified fruit wine or ice wine)

1. In a saucepan over medium heat, warm the cream, sugar, and salt, stirring occasionally, until bubbles form around the edges or it reaches 170°F on your digital thermometer.

2. Remove from the heat, allow the cream to cool slightly, and stir in the wine.

3. Cover the mixture with a lid and refrigerate overnight. Then, following the directions on your ice cream maker, freeze the mixture until scoopable.

Dead Frog Brewery

#1 27272 Gloucester Way, Langley, V4W 4A1; 1-888-856-1055
deadfrog.ca

"Nothing goes down like a cold dead frog!" That phrase makes me smile every time I hear it. Dead Frog is the original craft brewery in the Fraser Valley—Derrick and Donna Smith and their family have been making beer in Langley with some very cheeky branding since 2006, way before it was cool. They've weathered many storms, but have always stayed true to themselves and their brand, and they now offer a fantastic selection of microbrews.

In the heart of the Gloucester Industrial Park, Dead Frog brews, bottles, and pours 6 days a week (it's closed on Sundays). You can drop in to visit the brewery, take a tour, sample a flight, meet the brewmaster, buy a case of cans or bottles, or fill your growler to go. Dead Frog is probably best known for The Classic, a smooth, easy-drinking

Growler

A growler is a 64-ounce container made specifically to transport beer you can only buy on tap. It is airtight, is usually made from glass or stainless steel, and allows you to take home draft beer from a brewery or taphouse without sacrificing any of its quality. And a grunt? It's a half growler, of course!

nut brown ale with flavors of chocolate and espresso (yes, really!). The brewery has a long track record of experimenting with fruit beer, of which I am a fan. They've done a lime and black pepper lager, a tropical fruit ale with notes of mango and passion fruit, and a blood orange bock. Brewmaster Steve Black loves to have fun with dark beer and has offered creations like their Commander Imperial Stout with sweet notes of oak, molasses, and whiskey, and the Nutty Uncle Peanut Butter Stout, which is actually brewed with cocoa beans and peanut butter! Their offerings change regularly, as does their availability in liquor stores, so check the website often for updates.

Dead Frog Beer Dip with Sausage

This is one of my dips that I make for casual parties, served with corn chips or soft pretzels for dipping. I have also been known to scoop leftover dip on top of a baked potato.

Makes about 3 cups

2 Tbsp unsalted butter + more for baking dish

½ cup finely chopped onion

1 clove garlic, minced

1 bottle Dead Frog nut brown ale

2 Tbsp Dijon mustard

1 package (8 oz) cream cheese, cubed

4 cups grated sharp white cheddar

Hot sauce

½ lb smoked Appetizer Sausage from Bonetti Meats (page 70), cut into ½-inch pieces

Corn chips, to serve

1. Butter the inside of an 8-inch round baking dish or cast iron pan and preheat your oven to 350°F.

2. In a medium-size saucepan over medium-high heat, melt the butter and sauté the onions until they begin to soften. Add the garlic and cook for 2 minutes, until translucent. Add the beer, the mustard, and then the cream cheese, stirring constantly to melt the cream cheese. Add the cheddar and hot sauce to taste, stirring to combine and adjusting the temperature so it doesn't scorch. After about 15 minutes, when the mixture is smooth, stir in the sausage. Pour the dip into the baking dish and bake for about 25 minutes, until bubbly. Remove from the oven and serve warm with corn chips for dipping.

3. This dip can be prepared and refrigerated in an airtight container up to 4 days in advance and baked right before you're ready to serve it. Leftovers can be refrigerated for up to a week and eaten cold or rewarmed.

Chef Brian Misko

Can be found at: House of Q and markets, trade shows, and specialty stores all over BC. If you're lucky, you can also catch him teaching classes at Well Seasoned (see page 107).
houseofq.ca

Since its humble beginnings in Brian and Corinne Misko's kitchen in 2007, House of Q, a Langley-based BBQ business, has become a bit of a household name. Brian's love of all things BBQ and a penchant for all things local brought him to create their flagship product, the international award–winning Apple Butter BBQ Sauce. It all started when Brian simmered 40 pounds of local apples with molasses, brown sugar, cinnamon, and a little rum—to name just a few of the ingredients. Apple Butter BBQ Sauce goes with almost anything you can put on your BBQ and is available at specialty food stores and markets all over Canada. You can also find Brian and Corinne competing at BBQ competitions, participating in home shows, or teaching classes all over North America. Brian says that when it comes to choosing local, the equation is simple: "Meet the person who grows or raises your food and it simply tastes better, and at the same time, it's better for you." And, since Brian is a BBQ pitmaster, he naturally loves to feature as much local and seasonal product on his grill as possible.

When it comes to meat, he's a bit of a BBQ traditionalist—low and slow, cooked over charcoal or wood is the only way to go—but when it comes to soups and sides, Brian's creativity really shines through. In his opinion, "The most important tool you can have in your kitchen is simply a willingness to try. The inquisitiveness to re-create the fabulous dish you have seen or tasted or to add an off-recipe ingredient 'just to see' what it will be like is the best tool one could have." I think that without that sense of adventure in the kitchen, the House of Q would never have gotten started—and what a loss that would have been!

Pulled Turkey Sandwiches with Cabbage, Radicchio, and Apple Slaw

Local turkey isn't just for Thanksgiving! Turkey thighs cook up succulent and moist, and in this recipe, they soak up all of the fantastic smokiness and get sweet and savory flavors first from the dry rub and then from the BBQ sauce. The slaw is meant to be piled high on top of the turkey on the sandwich. The local Granny Smith apples and apple cider in the slaw cut the richness of the turkey meat and make a fantastic marriage with the Apple Butter BBQ Sauce. This sandwich from Chef Brian is a great twist on classic pulled pork. You might never go back to pork once you have had a pulled turkey sandwich!

Makes about 24 sandwiches

Pulled Turkey

6–8 lb boneless turkey thighs

¾ cup House of Q House Rub

Apple wood chips, in foil packets

24 French dip rolls, sliced

House of Q Apple Butter BBQ Sauce

Cabbage and Radicchio Slaw

12–15 cups shredded green cabbage

1 head radicchio, shredded

2 Granny Smith apples, peeled and grated

1 cup mayonnaise

½ cup apple cider vinegar

2 Tbsp sugar

1 tsp pepper (or to taste)

1. For the turkey, place the thighs in a foil tray and generously season with the dry rub. Prepare your grill for indirect cooking on medium heat. Place a foil packet of wood chips under the grill grate on the hot side of the grill. Place the foil tray of turkey on the cooler side, close the lid, and allow the turkey to smoke for 2 to 3 hours, changing the wood chip packets as they burn and turn to ash.

2. Check the turkey with an instant-read digital thermometer every hour, and when the turkey reaches 150°F, cover with foil and continue cooking. Checking every 40 minutes or so, you want to continue to cook it until the internal temperature has reached 195°F (allow about 2 hours for this). At that point, the turkey is ready to be removed from the grill. Allow the turkey to rest and cool enough to handle. Pour off some of the liquid in the pan into a bowl and reserve. Using two forks, or your hands if you prefer, pull/shred the turkey, removing and discarding bones, cartilage, and any inedible bits as you work. Pour some of the reserved pan juices back onto the shredded turkey to add flavor and moisture to the mixture. Re-season with more of the BBQ dry rub as required.

3. While the turkey is cooling, prepare the slaw. Mix the cabbage, radicchio, and apples together in a serving bowl. In a separate bowl, whisk together the mayonnaise, vinegar, sugar, and pepper. About 1 hour before you plan to eat, pour the dressing on the vegetables, mix well to combine, and transfer to the refrigerator to keep cool. If you add the dressing too early, the vegetables will start to get a bit soggy.

4. To assemble a sandwich, place a generous portion of the pulled turkey onto the bottom half of the sliced buns. Add a squeeze of BBQ sauce and a generous pile of the dressed slaw. Put the top of the buns on and serve.

How to Prepare a Foil Packet for Smoking

Soak your favorite variety of wood chips in a bowl of water for about 30 minutes. Put several generous handfuls onto the middle of a 2- × 2-foot sheet of heavy-duty aluminum foil. Fold all four ends of the aluminum foil together to make a burrito-type pouch filled with the soaked chips.

Turn the pouch over and, with the tip of a knife, poke about ten holes in the bottom of it. Lift the grate of your preheated grill and drop the pouch over part of the burner or flame. When the pouch starts to smoke, you're ready to grill. You want to keep the lid closed and the temperature low while your food smokes. When the smoke runs out, if you want to add more, simply add another pouch, but remember, it is easy to get too much smoke on the food, which can make it taste a bit acrid. Less is generally more while you are learning how to balance it all.

Woods like apple, cherry, maple, and pecan tend to provide a bit of a sweeter smoke, while mesquite and hickory can be quite strong. Wood chips are readily available at specialty food stores, hardware stores, and lumber yards. Just make sure the chips you're using are untreated wood—you want smoke, not a bunch of burning chemicals

Chef Chris Roper

Can be found at: The Fat Cow and Oyster Bar,
#4 20178 – 96th Ave., Langley, V1M 0B2; 778-298-0077
thefatcow.ca

I first met Chris when he was about 16 years old. He wanted to learn how to cook, so his mom, Sandra, brought him into Well Seasoned to take some classes. Over the next couple of years, Chris took more classes and fell in love with being in the kitchen. His family encouraged his interest in the culinary arts, and he eventually decided he wanted to be a chef. After he graduated from high school, Chris enrolled in culinary school at Vancouver Community College and the rest, as they say, is history.

Chris honed his skills, learned the ropes, made friends with local producers, winemakers, and other chefs, paid his dues, made some mistakes, and started to build a great reputation for himself. Then he met his wife, Emmy, and shortly before they got married, Chris and Emmy opened their own restaurant—the Fat Cow and Oyster Bar in Langley, a West Coast–inspired, upscale casual restaurant with a small seasonal, seafood-centric menu. Chris takes tremendous pride in sourcing simple, fresh local ingredients and reimagining their potential. Giant steamer buckets of mussels and clams, sweet smoked beets, popcorn with pork cracklings, and house-churned butter on fresh corn bread are just a few of the menu items that keep me going back to the Fat Cow. Emmy keeps the front of house in order—the craft beer cold, the cocktail menu fresh, and the wine list loaded with local BC wines.

It makes me feel incredibly old, but at the same time, it does my heart good to see Chris thriving in his own kitchen, in a great restaurant he owns with his beautiful wife and their latest addition to the Fat Cow team, their son, Carter. I love knowing that Chris has a passion for local that was inspired, in some very small part, by what he might have learned in a class at Well Seasoned. I know his late mom would have been incredibly proud of her son, and I know his grandparents keep a close eye on his progress and beam with pride when I chat with them about how he's doing—he's doing a great job!

Beef Tartare with Cured Egg Yolk and Beet Sorbet

Steak tartare is a classic French dish, usually made from finely chopped raw beef and traditionally served with onions, capers, seasonings, a raw egg yolk, and rye bread. This is Chef Chris Roper's version—made, of course, with as many local ingredients as possible, so this recipe would be a good one to make after you've visited a selection of Langley producers. One of Chef Chris's primary purveyors is Rondriso Farms (page 214) in Surrey, and in this dish, he gets to show off the fine produce, eggs, and beef he gets there. This might be the "cheffiest" recipe in this book, as you need to start to prepare the cured egg yolk 6 days before you are going to serve it. Don't be overwhelmed or intimidated, though, because this recipe is actually quite simple and the components come together perfectly to make the dish extraordinary!

Cured Egg Yolk

1¾ cups kosher salt

1¼ cups sugar

4 large egg yolks

Beet Sorbet

6 Tbsp sugar

6 Tbsp water

1¼ cups beet juice (store-bought is fine)

2 Tbsp liquid glucose

2 tsp lemon juice

1 gelatin leaf

1. To make the cured egg yolk, combine the salt and sugar in a bowl. Place half the mixture evenly in the bottom of an 8-inch square glass baking dish. Make four divots in the mixture and place 1 egg yolk in each divot, being careful not to break the yolk. Gently sprinkle the remaining half of the salt and sugar mixture over the eggs. Tightly wrap with plastic wrap and place in the refrigerator for 4 days.

2. Preheat the oven to 150°F.

3. Remove the eggs from the salt. Brush off each egg yolk and gently wash under cold running water. The eggs will be firm and bright in color. Gently pat dry, place in a baking dish, and dry in the oven until opaque and the texture is firm, 2½ to 3 hours. Remove from the oven and let cool. If you can't get your oven as low as 150°F, you can dry them out in the dish in a warm, dark place, uncovered, for 2 days.

4. To make the beet sorbet, in a medium-size saucepan over medium heat, bring the sugar and water to a simmer, stirring occasionally, until the sugar is fully dissolved. Remove from the heat. Add the beet juice, liquid glucose, and lemon juice.

5. In a small cup, soften the gelatin leaf by soaking it in cold water, about 10 minutes. Squeeze out any excess water from the gelatin leaf and add it to the beet mix. Return the saucepan to the heat until the gelatin is fully dissolved, then remove from the heat again and cool completely.

Beef Tartare

½ lb beef tenderloin

2 tsp finely minced shallots

2 tsp finely minced capers

2 tsp finely minced cornichons

2 tsp chopped anchovies
(about 2 small)

2 Tbsp chervil leaves or
chopped flat-leaf parsley +
more for garnish

2 Tbsp grainy mustard

Salt and pepper

To Assemble

1/4 cup crème fraîche

12 seedy crackers

6. Churn the mixture in an ice cream maker (that has been frozen for use) until it reaches a smooth, thick consistency. Transfer to an airtight container in the freezer for at least 3 hours or up to 4 weeks.

7. To make the tartare, place the beef in the freezer to firm up. The meat will chill from the outside in. You want the surface to be frozen slightly and the inside chilled but not frozen. This should take about 30 minutes, depending on your freezer settings.

8. Once the beef is chilled, cut it into slices, then strips, then cubes; the finer the better.

9. In a small bowl, mix all the ingredients together and taste to check for seasoning.

10. To assemble the dish, first chill your plates. Remove them from the refrigerator right before assembly. Spread out half of the beef mixture along the curvature of the plate. Next, with a small spoon, drop dots of crème fraîche alongside and on top of the tartare. Remove the sorbet from the freezer, and with a small ice cream scoop, place two small scoops of beet sorbet on the plate. Garnish the beef with a few pieces of the fresh chervil or flat-leaf parsley and, finally, shave the cured egg yolk over the entire dish with a fine rasp or grater. Stick the crackers into the tartare so they're standing up. Serve immediately.

Consuming raw or undercooked meats, poultry, seafood, shellfish, eggs or unpasteurized dairy may increase your risk of foodborne illness.

Crispy Pork Belly (recipe on page 102)

Chef Carl Sawatsky

Can be found at: Well Seasoned,
#117 20353 — 64 Ave., Langley, BC V2N 1Y5; 604-530-1518
wellseasoned.ca

Carl Sawatsky's culinary passion was kindled at the age of 12, when he was put in charge of feeding his family when his mom went back to work. He soon realized that he had a knack for flavors and a flair for creativity and that he wanted to become a chef. Carl's cuisine is inspired by BC's beautiful landscape and diverse culture. He creates dishes with the West Coast in mind, using a variety of French and modern techniques and, of course, incorporating local food as often as possible into all of his dishes. He is the executive chef and cooking class instructor at Well Seasoned (page 107) in Langley.

Carl is a great family guy with a weakness for awesome knives. He is lots of fun to be around, has a great sense of humor, and is always experimenting with new ideas, new techniques, and new recipes—he'll try anything once. But when it comes to buying local and cooking with seasonal ingredients, Carl relies on the personal connection he has with the producers and farmers he gets to work with. Being able to share that connection with the students in Well Seasoned classes is incredibly important to Carl; he wants people to know where their food comes from. Farmers and chefs adapt—that's just part of the gig. Occasionally when Carl has found himself in a bind, short of ingredients or missing something entirely, a farmer friend has happily and willingly come to his aid. And when his farmer friends have struggled because of weather conditions and found themselves with 300 pounds of zucchini at their peak of ripeness with nowhere to send it, Carl has stepped up and found a way to put it all to good use. When farmers and chefs truly collaborate, magic happens, and Carl makes magic.

Crispy Pork Belly with Hazelnut Pistou and Beans

Chef Carl Sawatsky has an affinity for fresh local pork, especially from Johnston's (johnstons.ca), a family-run business in Chilliwack that's been around for over 80 years. Johnston's believe in treating their animals as well as they do their employees, and you can taste the care in every bite of their mouth-watering pork.

Cark's recipe for crispy pork belly is also great in its components; the pistou (pesto) can be used in so many other applications—tossed on fresh pasta, dolloped on freshly steamed asparagus, or slathered generously on a crostini. Don't let this recipe intimidate you. There are a lot of steps, but it is totally worth the effort! (But note that you need to soak the beans the night before you plan to eat this. Trout beans are asked for here but you can use any hearty beans that will stand up to cooking, such as navy beans.) (Recipe photo on page 100)

Serves 6

Beans
1½ cups uncooked trout beans

1 small yellow onion, diced

½ carrot, diced

½ stalk celery, diced

2 bay leaves

1 Tbsp extra virgin olive oil

½ tsp kosher salt

Pork Belly
2.2 lb pork belly (preferably center cut)

1 Tbsp fresh ground fennel seeds

½ Tbsp kosher salt

½ tsp pepper

1 large onion, cut into 5 rings

2 cups water

1. The night before you plan to cook this, soak the beans overnight in enough water to come up at least 2 inches above them.

2. The next day, preheat the oven to 300°F.

3. For the pork belly, score the skin of the pork belly about 1 inch deep in a crosshatch pattern. Rub the skin, getting into the cuts, with the fennel seeds, salt and pepper. In a baking dish just large enough to hold the pork, lay down the onions so that the pork has a place to sit. Place the pork onto the onions skin side up. Add the water to the pan, cover tightly with aluminum foil, and bake the pork belly for 3 hours.

4. Meanwhile, cook the beans. Discard the water from the beans and place the beans in a large saucepan with the vegetables and bay leaves. Add enough water to cover everything, plus an extra ½ inch, and bring to a simmer over medium heat. Slowly simmer the beans, uncovered, over medium heat and add more hot water as needed to keep the beans submerged. The beans should take about 1½ hours to cook. Once the beans are tender but not falling apart, add the olive oil and salt to the water.

5. For the pistou, bring a medium-size saucepan of salted water to a boil and blanch the kale (or mustard greens) for 10 seconds. Cool under cold running water, then squeeze out the water. Roughly chop the greens.

6. In a blender, add in all of the ingredients in the order listed, but end with the greens. Blend until the ingredients are combined but not smooth—the chunkier the better. Set aside until the pork is done.

Pistou

2 packed cups Glorious Organics (page 62) kale or mustard greens

⅓ cup extra virgin olive oil

¼ cup cold water

3 Tbsp champagne vinegar

⅓ cup local hazelnuts, toasted and peeled + more for garnish

½ cup loosely packed basil

½ cup loosely packed flat-leaf parsley

1 tsp lemon zest

1 Tbsp lemon juice

1 clove garlic

½ tsp kosher salt

7. To check if the pork belly is done, stick a knife into the thickest part; it should go in easily and come out easily, like a warm knife through butter. When the pork is tender, remove it from the oven, and turn on the broiler. When the broiler reaches its highest temperature, transfer the pork to the top third of your oven. The pork skin will react to the high heat and start to puff after a few minutes. Keep an eye on it, but make sure to allow the pork skin to do its thing and puff up for you. If it doesn't puff enough, the skin will be tough and not tender and crunchy. This should take about 5 minutes. Immediately pull it out of the oven when the skin has all puffed up or before it starts to color too much and burn—it will be dark golden and kind of bubbly looking. Allow it to rest for 5 minutes before slicing.

8. To serve, slice the pork belly into six even pieces. Place about 1 cup of the beans with their liquid in the bottom of each of six bowls, making sure to pile the beans up to make a place for the pork belly to sit. Place a piece of pork belly on top of the beans, then spoon some of the pistou around the pork belly. Garnish with more toasted hazelnut pieces.

Chef Dan Trites

Can be found at: Ignite Café,
#102 5499 – 203rd Street, Langley, V3A 1W1; 604-724-8670
ignitecafe.ca

Chef Dan Trites and his wife, Angie, are the owners of Ignite Café in Langley, one of the Fraser Valley's best-known boutique cafés. The atmosphere at Ignite is relaxed and casual, and the offerings are always seasonal and entirely dependent on the whim of the chef, but one thing is contant: Dan always serves the hottest soup in town! You know how the soup is tepid at some restaurants? Not at Ignite. I'm pretty sure Ignite got its name from the temperature of the soup—it's fantastic!

Everything at Ignite is fresh, made from scratch, and features as many local ingredients and producers as possible. On the menu at Ignite, you will always find locally made fresh bread, cheeses from Farm House Natural Cheeses (page 191) in Agassiz, meat from Bonetti Meats (page 70), seafood from 1 Fish 2 Fish, and tons of veggies, herbs, and specialty ingredients from the farms and farm markets in the area. And wine, lots of BC wine—and, of course, craft beer. Make a reservation for dinner; if you're looking for lunch, check the website, as they open only occasionally at midday. Once you're settled at your table and looking at the menu, it might be hard to figure out where to start, but the ending is always easy to determine—try the Chocolate Peanut Butter Cheesecake. It's a game changer.

Psssst: If you don't find yourself in Langley and are anxious to try some of Chef Dan's fantastic food, you can find his fresh and frozen soups, sides, and entrées for sale at Nature's Pickin's in Abbotsford (page 142). His newest venture, Fireside Kitchen, provides grab-and-go meal solutions that are made from scratch with local ingredients. Dinner just got easier. Thanks, Dan.

Ignite West Coast Hot Pot

Chef Dan Trites makes this with the best seafood available and serves it with generous chunks of toasted garlic bread to soak up the broth.

Serves 4

½ white onion, cut in half and sliced

1 red bell pepper, sliced

2 Tbsp unsalted butter

1 Tbsp olive oil

1 Tbsp minced garlic

2 Tbsp chopped basil

¼ tsp dried red chili flakes

¼ tsp fennel seeds

¼ tsp dried dill

¼ tsp dried basil

12 nugget potatoes, cooked al dente

8 freshly shucked oysters

2 lb fresh mussels, debearded and washed

2 lb fresh manila clams, washed

1 lb BC spot prawns (in season)

1 lb halibut, skin off and cut into 4 portions

1½ cups dry white wine

1 can/bottle (13 oz) strained tomatoes or passata

¼ cup Pernod

Juice of 1 lemon

1 small bunch flat-leaf parsley, chopped, for garnish

1. In a large stockpot over medium-high heat, sweat the onions and bell peppers in the butter and olive oil, about 8 minutes. Stir in the garlic, fresh basil, and all of the dried herbs. Add the potatoes, oysters, mussels, clams, prawns, and halibut. Stir to combine. Add the wine, tomatoes, Pernod, and lemon juice. Gently stir and cover with a lid.

2. Cook, covered, over medium heat for about 10 minutes, until all of the shells are open, the seafood is cooked through, and the potatoes are fork-tender.

3. Using a large ladle, remove the seafood from the pot, dividing it evenly into four large bowls. Once the seafood is distributed, equally ladle out the remaining liquid and serve immediately, garnished with a sprinkling of flat-leaf parsley.

Other Places to Visit

Blacksmith Bakery

#102 9190 Church St., Fort Langley, V1M 2R6; 604-371-0181

No doubt about it, Chef Stephan Schigas serves some of the best pastries in the region. The menu is loaded with freshly baked croissants, sticky buns, and Viennoiserie, not to mention hearty soups made with as many fresh local ingredients as possible. And you must try the pizza—you are going to love it! (blacksmithbakery.ca)

Blackwood Lane Winery

25180 – 8th Ave., Langley, V4W 2G8; 604-856-5787

If you're touring wineries in South Langley, leave yourself time to visit Blackwood Lane. Blackwood Lane boasts some of BC's most premium red wines. Cellar tours are available on weekends (check the website for costs) and require advance booking. You can sip and sample in the tasting room or enjoy their wine with a snack on their beautiful patio. (blackwoodlanewinery.com)

The Glass House Estate Winery

23449 0 Ave., Langley, V2Z 2X3; 604-533-1212

Wow! This place is amazing, a definite stop for your visit to the Fraser Valley. Opened in mid-2017, this is a stunningly beautiful facility on a 40-acre vineyard in the most southern part of Langley. So far south in fact, the family likes to joke that they are Canada's closest winery to Napa. Enjoy a flight, a glass, or a bottle with a charcuterie board or some of their custom-smoked West Coast seafood. Good luck tearing yourself away—you are going to want to move in! (glasshouseestatewinery.com)

OSSO Lunchroom

#703 20381 – 62nd Ave., Langley, V3A 5E6; 778-278-0220

Chef Sean Bone's bistro serves up a fantastic breakfast, wicked good pizza, and a great assortment of fresh, seasonal, locally sourced food. They open and close early—they don't do dinner—so plan to visit early in the day or for a late-afternoon happy hour. (ossolunchroom.com)

Roots and Wings Distillery

7897 – 240th St., V1M 3P9; 604-371-2268

Two words: vodka and whiskey. Made in Langley's very first distillery, the spirits are created using potatoes and corn grown on the property. Go visit. (rootsandwingsdistillery.ca)

The Water Shed Arts Café

20349 – 88th Ave., Langley, V1M 2K5; 604-882-0651

Three minutes off of Highway 1, you will meet Chef Jenn, Naomi (who wears many hats), and their team of bakers and baristas. The food is killer, the coffee is great, kombucha is available on tap, and there's always local art on the wall and occasionally live music in the evenings. This is a great place to visit if you are vegan or vegetarian; they have lots of tasty options and even bake their own bread. (watershedartscafe.com)

Well Seasoned

#117 20353 – 64th Ave., Langley, V2Y 1N5; 604-530-1518

This gourmet food store is MY place and I might be slightly partial, but it is awesome. It's a true foodies' paradise, loaded with food, spices, and ingredients made by local and small-scale producers. It's full of stuff you won't find anywhere else. Oh, and there are cooking classes offered daily, taught by some of the most talented chefs in BC! (wellseasoned.ca)

Wendel's Bookstore & Café

9233 Glover Rd., Langley, V1M 2S5; 604-513-2238

This store in Fort Langley has been selling books and serving pie since 1997. Wendel's is an institution in the Fort. Open for breakfast, lunch, and dinner 7 days a week, it has an espresso bar, a great wine and beer list, and a full menu that features lots of locally sourced ingredients and an impressive selection of house-made desserts. Wendel's is known locally as *the* place to go for great gluten-free treats. (wendelsonline.com)

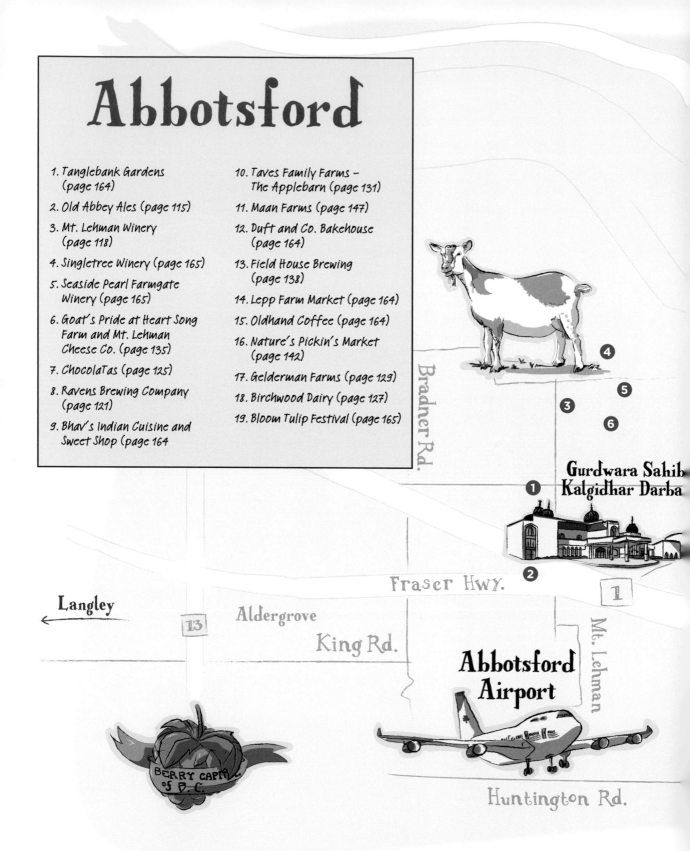

Abbotsford

Bradner Rd.

Gurdwara Sahib
Kalgidhar Darba

Fraser Hwy.

Langley

Aldergrove

King Rd.

Mt. Lehman

Abbotsford
Airport

BERRY CAPITAL
of B.C.

Huntington Rd.

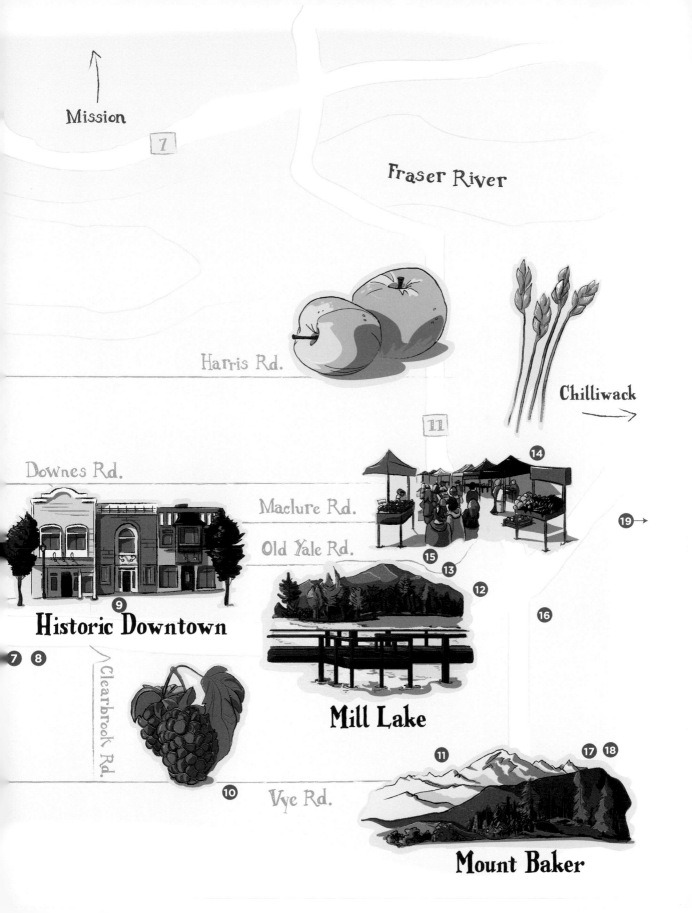

Mission

Fraser River

Harris Rd.

Chilliwack

Downes Rd.

Maclure Rd.

Old Yale Rd.

Historic Downtown

Clearbrook Rd.

Mill Lake

Vye Rd.

Mount Baker

Abbotsford

bbotsford, often referred to as Abby by people in the Valley, calls itself the City in the Country. It's a fitting nickname for this diverse, multicultural city that about 150,000 people call home. Tucked into the heart of the Fraser Valley between Sumas Mountain, the Township of Langley, and Chilliwack, Abbotsford is a fantastic place to visit. It has some of the richest farmland in the region, and because of that it's known regionally as BC's raspberry capital. In fact, on a warm summer day in July as you drive along the rural roads, if you open your windows, turn your radio down, and slow down, you can actually smell the raspberries in the fields. You probably just asked yourself, why do I need to turn the radio down to smell something? When you want to heighten one of your senses, you need to dull another. Try it! Close your eyes the next time you taste something—it's fascinating.

From just about anywhere in Abbotsford, on a clear day you will have a majestic view of Mt. Baker (in Washington State) and the Coast Mountains to the north. The Abbotsford International Airport (YXX) is just 2 miles south of the city center, opening access to visitors from all over Canada. It's a great alternative to Vancouver's very busy YVR—you won't believe what a different experience it is to travel through this airport.

Abbotsford's agricultural roots attracted people from all over the world looking to settle in Canada, and as such it has become one of the most multicultural cities in the Valley. The Mennonite Heritage Museum, open to the public and free to visit, is a fine example of the contribution immigrants can make to a community. But what I find most interesting is that Abbotsford is home to the oldest-standing Sikh temple

(Gurdwara) in Canada (and it's well worth a visit). In 1905, some of the first employees at the old mill at Mill Lake in the center of Abbotsford were Sikhs who brought their culture, food, and religion with them. Since then, they've made a significant impact on the community, including the introduction of their traditional cuisine. As you explore the area, you'll come across some of the best Indian restaurants and sweet shops in the country. If you're unfamiliar with Indian sweets, start by trying gulab jamun, which is kind of like a dense donut that has been soaked in a flavorful syrup. Sometimes they're even garnished with real gold. They're best accompanied by a strong cup of coffee or chai. But don't forget to grab a handful of napkins on your way out—Indian sweets are sticky!

Tourist information: **tourismabbotsford.ca**
Facebook: **@TourismAbbotsford**
Instagram: **@tourismabbotsford**
Twitter: **@TourismAbby**

The old part of downtown Abbotsford has recently enjoyed a bit of a revival—buildings and homes from the early 1900s have been renovated and turned into quaint cafés, boutiques, and independent shops. It's a great place to spend the day poking around! The farmers market runs on Sunday mornings in the historic town center and is a great place to connect with locals and farmers in the heart of the city. Visit the Tourism Abbotsford website for events at the Tradex at Abbotsford Airport and events at the Abbotsford Centre, as there is always a lot happening at both locations. Plan to visit Abbotsford often. It's one of those places where you discover something new every time you turn around.

(PS: If you want to score extra points with Mom on Mother's Day, check out the Tulip Festival's website (abbotsfordtulipfestival.ca) early in the year to buy tickets for this amazing event. They sell out unbelievably quickly, so don't delay!)

Old Abbey Ales

#1A 30321 Fraser Hwy., Abbotsford, V4X 1T3; 604-607-5104
oldabbeyales.com

Old Abbey Ales is just a quick 1-minute detour off of Highway 1 at the Mt. Lehman exit. In their unassuming light industrial–type location, they produce a huge variety of beer. When I visited, there were more than 20 on tap. Old Abbey sells commercial brewing equipment and uses their demonstration brewery to teach other brewmasters, and customers can see the whole brewery from the bar, which is kind of cool. The tasting bar is big, giving you plenty of room to peruse the giant menu boards to decide which ones you want to try. Because of the teaching aspect involved in the business, the choice of beer on tap is seemingly endless.

Old Abbey's beers are made in the Belgian style. As their name suggests, they specialize in ales, but they've recently won awards and critical acclaim for their Sour Raspberry beer, brewed with barley, wheat, hops, and, of course, fresh Abbotsford raspberries. Sour beer has been around forever and is made intentionally sour to appeal to the palates of more sophisticated beer fans who are maybe a little bored of the same old, same old. As with fine wine, a lot of finesse is required to make great beer, especially sour beer, and since the Fraser Valley is Canada's top raspberry-producing region, it only made sense to make a crisp and refreshing beer featuring one of the area's best-known ingredients.

The atmosphere at Old Abbey is like a pub in a warehouse. Seats are available at the bar or at high-top tables, there is fresh popcorn popping, and on a warm day the overhead garage doors are open to the parking lot. You can fill your growler, buy cans or bottles of beer to go, or just enjoy a flight with friends.

Summer Herb Salad with Old Abbey IPA and Orange Vinaigrette

In the late spring and early summer, fresh herbs are abundant and inexpensive. This is a salad I created as a great way to take advantage of the seasonal bounty. The hoppy bitterness of the Old Abbey IPA, combined with the freshness of the orange and the sweetness of the honey, makes these greens sing! The fresh herbs and leaves in this mix are delicate and will wilt quickly, so make sure to serve the salad immediately once it's dressed. Try substituting the herbs with your personal favorites or whatever is in season.

Serves 6

Vinaigrette
¼ cup Old Abbey Belgian Tripel IPA

1 Tbsp minced shallots

½ clove garlic, minced

2 Tbsp white balsamic vinegar

1 tsp orange zest

1 Tbsp honey

1 tsp grainy mustard

¼ cup extra virgin olive oil

Salt and pepper

Salad
1 small bunch dill, heavy stems discarded

1 small bunch basil, leaves only

1 small bunch mint, leaves only

1 bunch flat-leaf parsley, leaves only

1 bunch cilantro, leaves only

1 small clamshell or 2 small bunches (5 oz) arugula leaves

1 head butter lettuce

Salt and pepper

¼ cup toasted, flaked almonds

Edible flowers, to garnish (optional)

1. For the vinaigrette, in a small bowl, whisk the beer with the shallots, garlic, orange zest, vinegar, honey, and mustard. Gradually add the oil in a thin stream, whisking constantly. Season the vinaigrette with salt and pepper. (The vinaigrette can be stored in an airtight container in the refrigerator for up to 3 days.)

2. For the salad, wash and spin dry all of the herb leaves. Gently tear the dill, basil, and mint leaves into a medium-size bowl, and add the whole leaves of parsley and cilantro. Add the arugula. Tear the larger butter lettuce leaves into the salad and leave the smaller ones whole. Toss to combine.

3. Dress with the vinaigrette, season with salt and pepper to taste, and garnish with the toasted almonds and edible flowers (if using). Serve immediately.

Mt. Lehman Winery

5094 Mt. Lehman Rd., Abbotsford, V4X 1Y3; 604-746-2881
mtlehmanwinery.com

Vern and Charleen Siemens opened Mt. Lehman Winery in 2009, and I swear they have one of the most stunning views in the entire Fraser Valley (and believe me, the bar is high when it comes to stunning views in the Valley). Snow-covered Mt. Baker looms in the distance, and if you stretch your arms out, you can almost reach the farms and rolling hills of the entire region from right there on the crest of the hill. It is truly spectacular and makes it easy to understand immediately why Vern and Charleen love it there so much.

Best known for its pinot noir, Mt. Lehman Winery has about 17 acres of vineyard growing a variety of grapes. Their grapes are supplemented by fruit brought in from the Okanagan Valley, allowing Vern to take full advantage of the very best grapes from the two growing seasons to blend his beautiful wines. In the last decade, Mt. Lehman and Vern have won numerous awards, including the very prestigious Lieutenant General's Award of Excellence.

When you visit Mt. Lehman Winery, make sure there's plenty of room in the trunk of your car. You're going to want to buy plenty of wine to take home. With a tempting array that includes merlot, gewürztraminer, pinot gris, syrah, and rosé, there's something to suit every palate, picnic basket, and dinner table.

Pinot noir is known as the heartbreak grape. It requires more care and attention than other varietals, and if the vines aren't managed properly, the juice will be flat and lacking in depth and flavor. A good pinot requires a ton of finesse from both the grower and the winemaker, so an award like the Lieutenant General's Award of Excellence, given to a winery producing fantastic pinot noir from fruit grown locally in the Fraser Valley, where the climate and terroir can be consistently less than cooperative, is a more significant achievement than many would think.

Rack of Lamb with Blueberry Reduction

This recipe by Chef Dez (page 150) is great in the fall and winter when local blueberries aren't in season, so make sure you freeze some when they are so you have them on hand when you want to make this dish in February.

Serves 4

2 racks (each about 12 oz) fresh local lamb, frenched (see sidebar)

2 Tbsp vegetable oil

Salt and pepper

½ cup Mt. Lehman pinot noir

2 cups fresh or frozen blueberries

2½ tsp sugar

2 tsp beef stock paste

2–3 Tbsp whipping cream

Roasting Guide for Lamb

You'll get the most accurate reading with a digital thermometer.

115°F to 120°F = rare

120°F to 125°F = medium-rare

130°F to 135°F = medium

140°F to 145°F = medium-well

150°F+ = well done

160°F+ = order a pizza

1. Preheat the oven to 450°F.

2. Oil the lamb racks with 1 Tbsp of the oil, and season them with salt and pepper.

3. Heat a heavy-bottomed frying pan over medium heat. Add the remaining 1 Tbsp oil to the pan and sear the racks on both sides and the ends to form a nice golden crust. This will take about 5 minutes total.

4. Transfer the lamb to a wire rack set in a roasting pan and roast in the oven for about 15 minutes. This will give you a doneness of medium-rare, but you can cook to your desired doneness level with the use of a digital thermometer (see the roasting guide in the sidebar). Once you're happy with the doneness of the meat, remove it from the oven and transfer to a cutting board, tent it loosely with foil, and allow it to rest while you prepare the sauce.

5. Place the roasting pan on the stovetop over medium-high heat and deglaze the pan with a generous splash, about 2 Tbsp, of the wine, scraping all of the brown bits off the bottom of the pan with a wooden spoon. Add the remaining wine, berries, sugar, and beef paste to the pan and bring to a boil, still over medium-high heat, stirring constantly. Once everything is fully combined and the beef paste has dissolved, turn down the heat and, with the back of the wooden spoon, start to break up the berries a bit, but don't mash them completely. After the sauce has simmered for about 10 minutes, mash the rest of the berries with a potato masher. Stir to combine.

6. With a fine-mesh sieve, strain this sauce into a bowl, then return the sauce to the pan. Discard the pulp left in the strainer.

7. To the sauce, over medium heat, add the cream and reduce the sauce until it is thick and syrupy. Taste and adjust seasoning with more salt and pepper if required.

8. Slice the lamb rack into chops by cutting between each of the bones. Ladle the pan sauce over the chops and serve immediately.

＊⟩⟩𝈫

A frenched lamb rack simply has had the meat, fat, and membranes that connect the individual rib bones removed, giving the rack a clean look for a more elegant presentation. If you aren't comfortable doing it, ask your butcher, as they're usually quite happy to do it for you.

𝈫⟨⟨＊

Ravens Brewing Company

2485 Townline Rd., Abbotsford, V2T 6L6; 604-758-1557
ravensbrewing.com

Ravens Brewing Company opened in July 2015 and was borne from a ground-to-glass philosophy. Owner Paul Sweeting finds much of his inspiration in the agriculture surrounding Abbotsford, and he and his team work to showcase as many local ingredients as possible in the creation of a West Coast, European-inspired style of beer. This is a philosophy I can totally embrace!

While all of the choices at Ravens are excellent, there were two that really stood out for me when I visited on a hot summer day: Ravens Raspberry Hefeweizen, a wheat ale made with fresh local raspberries that is available only seasonally, and the Farmhouse Cider, a dry and crisp cider with just enough sweetness made from Taves Family Farms (page 131) apples. Knowing that the Taves's Applebarn is just a few miles away, I somehow felt almost righteous in the consumption of cider, knowing that I was supporting two great local businesses at the same time! That feeling of righteousness was so strong, I had a second glass just to make sure it was real! I am seriously looking forward to visiting the brewery closer to Christmas so I can try the Hot Chocolate Porter, a dark beer made with real cocoa nibs. Beer and chocolate, color me sold!

The tasting room at Ravens isn't huge, and for me that adds to its attraction. The word "quaint" comes to mind for me—not dainty quaint, but warm and welcoming, and certainly more intimate than some of the other tasting rooms I've visited in my time. We had a great experience and spent time chatting with the very friendly staff about the business while we enjoyed our flight and waited for our growlers to be filled. You can buy beer to go from the tasting room in bombers or you can fill your grunt or your growler.

Ravens Brewing Farmhouse Cider and Squash Soup

You can fill your growler of Farmhouse Cider at Ravens Brewing and enjoy a glass at home while you prepare this soup for dinner. Kabocha is one of my favorite squash for soup, but feel free to swap it out with pumpkin or butternut—this may be my recipe, but it's yours to play with. The sweet richness of the vanilla yogurt stirred into the soup really adds to the depth, but feel free to garnish it with plain yogurt, sour cream, or some roasted pumpkin seeds. This soup freezes really well without the yogurt and can be dressed up for a dinner party or transported in a thermos for a fall picnic.

Serves 4 as a first course
or 2 as a main

1 Tbsp unsalted butter

1 medium-size kabocha
squash, peeled and diced

2 carrots, peeled and roughly
chopped

1 medium yellow onion,
roughly chopped

4 cups chicken or vegetable
stock

1½ cups Ravens Brewing
Farmhouse Cider

Salt

2 Tbsp maple syrup

¼ cup whipping cream

2 Tbsp Greek-style vanilla
yogurt or sour cream, for
garnish

¼ cup toasted pumpkin
seeds, for garnish

1. In a large saucepan over medium heat, melt the butter and sauté the squash, carrots, and onions for about 10 minutes, stirring to combine and to ensure they don't brown. Add the stock and cider to the saucepan, stirring to combine, and bring to a boil. Cover the pan and turn down the heat to low. Allow the soup to simmer for about 30 minutes, stirring occasionally.

2. Once the squash is soft and the carrots are fully cooked, use an immersion blender to purée the soup until smooth. (This can also be done in a blender or food processor; just be careful when puréeing hot liquids.) Season to taste with salt, stir in the maple syrup and cream, and warm through. Ladle into bowls and garnish with the yogurt and seeds. Serve immediately.

ChocolaTas

#101 31060 Peardonville Rd., Abbotsford, V2T 6K5; 1-877-668-8932
chocolatas.com

Wim Tas is an award-winning master chocolatier and a true culinary artist. Like any farm-fresh product, fresh chocolate, made with no preservatives, is meant to be enjoyed soon after it's made. Wim was trained at Belgium's most respected chocolate house, La Maison Wittamer, the exclusive supplier of chocolate to Belgian royalty. In 2002, Wim and his wife, Veve, immigrated to Canada to share their passion for chocolate with us. ChocolaTas had humble beginnings in Abbotsford, starting in their home, but the business quickly expanded. They now have a thriving shop in the heart of Granville Island Public Market in Vancouver as well as the shop and full production kitchen in Abbotsford. At ChocolaTas, you'll find a hard-to-resist, mouthwatering array of traditional-style chocolates handmade in small batches, including buttery caramels, nut-based fillings made with local nuts, and some super-interesting combinations like black pepper and mango, tomato and basil, and caramel with salt and rosemary. The flavors change seasonally at the whim of Wim. The contemporary packaging design and brilliant flavor combinations are really what set ChocolaTas apart. Because these chocolates are fresh, they have a short shelf life, so you're going to have to visit often!

Truffle-Stuffed Molten Chocolate Cakes

I created my first version of this recipe years ago for my dad, a true lover of chocolate—it is simple and super-rewarding. You can use your favorite plain or flavored truffle in the center. At ChocolaTas, they make a truffle with almond praline paste that is outstanding in this dessert.

Serves 4

3 Tbsp unsalted butter, at room temperature + more for buttering ramekins

3 Tbsp Dutch-process cocoa, for dusting

4 oz best-quality semi-sweet chocolate, chopped

1 Tbsp whipping cream

2 large eggs, at room temperature

¼ cup sugar

1 tsp pure vanilla extract

⅛ tsp salt

1 Tbsp all-purpose flour

6 ChocolaTas chocolate truffles, about 1 inch round

½ cup whipping cream, whipped and lightly sweetened, or vanilla ice cream, for serving

1. Preheat the oven to 400°F.

2. Generously butter six ovenproof 6 oz (¾ cup) ramekins and dust each well with cocoa powder. Place the prepared ramekins on a rimmed baking pan and prepare the filling.

3. In a small bowl over a small saucepan of simmering water (or in a double boiler), melt together the chocolate, whipping cream, and the 3 Tbsp butter, stirring to combine and to ensure your chocolate doesn't burn. When the mixture is smooth, set aside to cool for about 10 minutes at room temperature.

4. In a large bowl, place the eggs, sugar, vanilla, and salt. With an electric mixer on medium-high speed, beat until the mixture triples in volume and is very thick, about 5 minutes. Sift the flour over the egg mixture and, with a rubber spatula, fold the flour into the mixture. Then fold in the cooled chocolate/butter mixture and continue to fold until it is well mixed.

5. Pour the mixture into the prepared ramekins.

6. Drop one chocolate truffle into the center of each filled ramekin, pressing gently to submerge it in the batter. If it doesn't fully submerge, that's okay—it will sink as it bakes. Transfer the baking pan with the filled ramekins to the oven and bake for 9 to 10 minutes, just until the tops are set. Remove from the oven and let the cakes cool in the ramekins on a wire rack for about 5 minutes.

7. Run a sharp knife around the edge of each cake between the cake and the ramekin to loosen it and turn out onto individual serving plates. Or, if you're nervous about doing that, feel free to leave them in the ramekins; they are going to taste just as delicious. (Removing them from the ramekins just makes them a bit fancier.) Serve immediately with lightly sweetened whipped cream or vanilla ice cream.

Birchwood Dairy

1154A Fadden Rd., Abbotsford, V3G 1T9; 604-857-1315
birchwooddairy.com

Eating ice cream makes most people happy. From a cone, from a cup, or straight out of the carton with a spoon late at night, it doesn't much matter. But if you are going to indulge, it might as well be worth it! Len and Grace Krahn make sure it's worth it every time you dig into a tub of their fresh, hand-made frozen deliciousness! They started processing dairy in the 1980s, and while many things have

changed over the years, the quality and the pride in every scoop of Birchwood ice cream remain exactly the same.

Birchwood Dairy Farm is located on 220 acres of land on the beautiful Sumas Prairie in Abbotsford, where they milk about 125 cows and grow enough hay and silage (made from corn) to feed the herd all year, and turn their fresh dairy into more than 50 flavors of ice cream, sour cream, European-style yogurt, and various cheeses, including fresh cheddar curds—the really squeaky ones that are so much fun to eat.

While you sit at one of the picnic tables or on a blanket on the grass, enjoying your ice cream or frozen yogurt, you can relax and soak up the ambience of the country. If you time your visit between 3:30 and 5:00 p.m., you can watch the cows being milked. It's pretty cool, but keep in mind when you visit that Birchwood is a working farm. Cows that make delicious dairy for ice cream also make cow poop. The smell can be a little . . . umm . . . "strong" on a hot day, but hey, that's farm life! It's a great place to get up close and personal with where our food actually comes from. If you're traveling with kids, there are animals to pet and plenty of fun things to see, but keep an eye on them near the pens. You do not want to be tramping around barefoot, if you get what I'm saying!

Fresh Cheese Curd Panzanella Salad

A traditional panzanella salad is made with stale Italian bread soaked in water . . . But I think my recipe takes it to a whole new level—imagine the possibilities when you add the slightly charred bread to the fresh local cheese and fresh basil; my mouth waters just thinking about it. I could eat it literally every day. Cheese curds are fresh cheese that hasn't been pressed into a shape. They're milky and delicious, but quite plain tasting, which makes them perfect for this salad with its good strong garlicky dressing. They're also delicious cut into pieces and used on a grilled cheese sandwich. You'd better buy two packages, as they seem to disappear quite quickly!

Serves 4

2 cloves garlic, minced

1 handful basil leaves, chopped

2 Tbsp good-quality red wine vinegar

½ tsp Dijon mustard

½ tsp kosher salt

Pepper

½ cup extra virgin olive oil

2 lb ripe cherry or grape tomatoes, halved

¼ lb fresh Birchwood Dairy cheese curds, in 1-inch pieces

1 loaf crusty bread (ciabatta works well), in 1-inch slices

Small bundle fresh chives, minced

1. In a large bowl, whisk to combine the garlic, basil, red wine vinegar, Dijon, salt, pepper, and ¼ cup of the olive oil. Add the halved tomatoes and cheese curds and set aside.

2. Preheat a grill pan over medium-high heat. If you don't have a grill pan, you can use a toaster, a BBQ, or the broiler to toast the bread. The little charred bits you get from the pan or the BBQ make a great addition to the salad.

3. With a silicone pastry brush, generously brush both sides of the slices of bread with the remaining ¼ cup olive oil. Place the bread in the pan to grill, flipping occasionally, until grill marks appear and the bread is crisp, about 3 minutes per side. Set the bread aside on a cutting board to cool.

4. Once cool, cut the toasted bread slices into about 1-inch cubes and toss well with the rest of the salad. Season the mixture with more salt if needed and freshly cracked black pepper. Divide the panzanella between four large bowls and garnish with the minced chives. Serve immediately.

Fun Seasonal Substitution

In the middle of summer when peaches are fresh and ripe and amazing, try subbing sliced pitted peaches for the tomatoes and champagne vinegar for the red wine vinegar in this salad—it's a surprisingly glorious treat when the peaches are at their best.

Gelderman Farms

35805 Vye Rd., Abbotsford, V3G 1Z5; 604-864-9096
geldermanfarms.ca

Jerry and Audrey Gelderman raise pigs, and they're good at it! They both
grew up in the Fraser Valley, and over the past 30 years they have raised
their family there and turned their family farm into a diverse, thriving
business. While they don't have a farmgate store and you can't just pop
in when you're in the neighborhood (it's a working farm), you can
order your product online and pick it up at the farm or stop and see
them at one of the many farmers markets they frequent.

The pigs at Gelderman Farms are treated like royalty. They live in
spacious pens with sawdust beds and lots of room and freedom to run
around, and enjoy a vegetable-based diet that Jerry sources locally and
mills for them right on his farm. Like all Canadian pork, the
Geldermans' is sold free of growth hormones, but Jerry and Audrey go
one step further. If a pig falls ill and needs an antibiotic, it's removed
from the system and not sold until its system is completely clear of the antibiotics. I
think the extra time and attention the Geldermans give to the pigs result in a product
that is far superior to any imported pork, which has in turn led to a high demand for
their product. In partnership with a couple of local butchers and smokehouses, the
Geldermans also offer a fantastic range of value-added pork products like their
legendary thick-cut bacon, delicious ham, and ready-to-eat farmer's sausage.

As well as raising tasty, tasty pigs, they also grow blueberries, also sold at market,
and sell compost. They blend fresh manure with the used sawdust from the beds in
the pig pens and bring the temperature to above 150°F to kill weeds, seeds, and any
pathogens from the manure in the most natural way possible—which also removes the
odor—to create an all-natural, organic, and environmentally friendly compost sold as
Go Green Compost.

Warm Gelderman Bacon Salad with Blueberry Vinaigrette

Bacon makes everything better! Okay, maybe not quite everything, but in this case, the Gelderman bacon makes my salad fantastic—even if I do say so myself!

Serves 6 as a side

6 strips sliced Gelderman Farms bacon, cut into chunks

¼ cup extra virgin olive oil

1 small shallot, minced

¼ cup sherry vinegar

1 Tbsp grainy Dijon mustard

1 cup blueberries

1 lb local, seasonal salad greens

Salt and pepper

¼ cup crumbled feta

1. In a large frying pan, cook the bacon in the olive oil over medium-high heat until browned and crisp, about 6 minutes. Remove the pan from the heat and stir in the shallots, vinegar, and mustard, allowing the shallots to sweat in the residual heat of the oil. Continue to stir for another minute, then stir in the blueberries. Some of the blueberries will burst and their juices will mix into the vinaigrette; stir to combine.

2. Pour the warm vinaigrette and bacon chunks over the salad greens, season with salt and pepper, sprinkle with the feta, and serve right away.

Taves Family Farms —The Applebarn

333 Gladwin Rd., Abbotsford, V2T5Y1; 604-853-3108
tavesfamilyfarms.com

Late summer, early fall is when the Taves family opens their farm to
visitors. The Jonagolds are like little jewels hanging from the trees in the
10-acre orchard. In 1989, Loren Taves brought this variety of apple to
Canada from the Netherlands and planted the trees on a plot of land he
had been leasing. Several years later, as the orchard and Loren's apple
business grew, the owner of the land decided he wanted to sell, forcing
Loren to buy the land or give up his orchard, so he bought it! Loren
says farming is all about risk management—you have to have a good
marketing plan, a great product with a strong production process, and,
of course, finances. If they aren't all in sync, there's going to be trouble.
I would say Loren and Corinne and their eight children are doing
something right! They've built an incredible agritourism business on top
of their already successful greenhouse operation.

When you visit Taves Family Farms, you'll see that on one side of the road is the
Applebarn and across the street is a 185,000-square-foot greenhouse facility where the
Taveses grow those cute little sweet bell peppers, dark purple "barstock" eggplant,
English cucumbers, and tomatoes. (Yes, you read that correctly: the farm is split in
two by the road!) Most of what comes out of the greenhouse is sold wholesale and
ultimately into grocery stores and restaurants all over North America. The Applebarn
is open to the public.

You can see greenhouses all over the world, but what you can't experience
anywhere else is the fun and fabulousness in celebration of the humble apple at the
Applebarn. Apples don't grow in the grocery store, and sometimes it's just really great

to be reminded of that. From late August until the apples are gone, you can visit the Applebarn and pick your own. One of the first things you'll hear when you arrive at the Applebarn on a busy day is children laughing. They kill themselves laughing as they jump on the gigantic bouncing pillow, giggle like crazy as a goat nibbles on their shoelaces in the petting zoo, and squeal with delight as they finally find their way out of the corn maze or ride the slide in the playground. The Taves family has created a super-special place where you can spend a few hours or a whole day experiencing farm life. You can fire a custom-made pumpkin cannon or corn gun (this is where you hear the adults giggling) or watch in the cider mill as fresh Jonagolds are turned into cider. Inside the Applebarn Country Store you will find everything you could possibly want to take home—fresh apples, pies, pickles, produce, and, of course, fresh-pressed cider. If they have Honeycrisp apples available, grab a bag—they make the best apple crisp!

Good luck convincing the kids it's time to leave, but the good news is, you can come back. Often.

Mom Taves's Applecake

Corinne Taves's applecake is the best cake I have ever had for breakfast. The addition of the fresh apples somehow makes me feel less guilty about eating cake before 10:00 a.m. Try it and let me know how guilty you feel afterward.

Serves 10

Cake

1½ cups sugar

½ cup vegetable oil

½ cup applesauce

3 eggs

2 cups all-purpose flour

1½ tsp ground cinnamon

1 tsp baking soda

½ tsp salt

¼ tsp ground nutmeg

3 cups peeled and finely chopped ripe apples

Caramel Frosting

½ cup salted butter

1 cup brown sugar

¼ cup whole milk

2 cups icing sugar

1. Preheat the oven to 350°F. Line a 9- × 13-inch rimmed baking sheet with parchment paper.

2. For the cake, in a large bowl, mix together the sugar, oil, applesauce, and eggs.

3. Add the flour, cinnamon, baking soda, salt, and nutmeg and mix gently to combine. Do not overmix. Stir in the apples. Spoon the batter into the baking sheet and bake for 25 to 35 minutes, until brown and a toothpick inserted into the center comes out clean. Allow to cool while you make the caramel frosting.

4. For the frosting, in a medium-size saucepan over medium heat, melt the butter and stir in the brown sugar. Boil for 2 minutes, stirring constantly. Using a handheld whisk, whisk in the milk. Heat until boiling. Remove from the heat and place the bottom of the pan in a sink of cold water. As you gradually beat in the icing sugar, still using the handheld whisk, the frosting will thicken and become really smooth as it cools.

5. Spread the cooled frosting onto the cake, slice, and serve. (You don't need to let the frosting set before diving in.) The frosted cake can be stored in an airtight container for 2-3 days. Or so I've been told. I've never had any leftovers!

Goat's Pride Dairy at HeartSong Farm and Mt. Lehman Cheese Co.

30854 Olund Rd., Abbotsford, V4X 1Z9; 604-854-6261
goatspride.com
mtlehmancheese.ca

Goats are hilarious. I'm sure you've seen the videos on the Internet of baby goats being ridiculous and kung fu–kicking each other for sport. I can't be the only one who can't get enough of them. And that noise they make is fantastic! Goats are also incredibly charming, with very definite personalities. They're trusting, friendly, inquisitive, and fast—really, really fast!

At Goat's Pride Dairy, Peter and Jo-Ann Dykstra keep a herd of about 130 hooligans who roam freely on the 20 acres of lush grass, grazing, lazing, foraging, and just being cute—it's truly a goats' paradise. The Dykstras feed their goats a balanced diet of organic vegetables, fruit and veggie pulp, spent barley from a local organic brewery, and unsold organic bread from A Bread Affair, preventing it from going into the landfill. While the goats are in their barn, there's plenty of hay for them to nibble on and keep them warm, but the barn doors are always open and the goats come and go as they please. In their organically certified herd, Peter and Jo-Ann keep a mix to crossbreed, giving their milk great flavor and a depth of complexity you don't get from other dairies. Each goat produces about 1 ½ gallons of milk per day, and that fresh milk is then transformed into many delicious products limited only by the creativity of the producer, who just happens to be their son, Jason. Since the Dykstras started their goat milk production in 1993, market demand for goat dairy has increased exponentially. With more and more people experiencing allergies or sensitivities to cow dairy, goat products are a great hypoallergenic alternative.

Plan to stay a while to enjoy the farm. During your visit, you're invited to meet the herd, play with the "kids," and taste the products in the farm store. If you get a chance,

chat with Jo-Ann. She has some great anecdotes about goats to share and is a wealth of information about dairy. And no visit to Goat's Pride Dairy would be complete without a ride on their "goat-cart." Apparently it isn't just the goats that are hilarious at Goat's Pride; the Dykstras also have a great sense of humor. Actually, I think most farmers do.

Not far from the barns on HeartSong Farm is another thriving business . . .

In 2013, Jason Dykstra, Peter and Jo-Ann's son, started his own cheese company called Mt. Lehman Cheese Co. Jason started off making cheese with the milk from Goat's Pride, but as demand grew, he needed to source high-quality goat milk from other local goat farms so the milk produced at Goat's Pride could continue to be sold as organic milk and yogurt. Jason makes excellent cheese and currently offers nine different varieties, including Gozzarella (apparently the Dykstra sense of humor didn't skip a generation; this is a pasteurized goat milk cheese similar to a traditional mozzarella), blue cheese, goat cheddar, tomme (a hard-brined cheese), feta, and Frisky (a bloomed-rind, 21-day-aged brie-type cheese).

The most important part of your trip planning for Mt. Lehman Cheese and Goat's Pride Dairy is to pack the crackers. You're going to want to bring plenty so you can enjoy the cheese properly. Oh, and that winery you stopped at earlier in the day? I hope you grabbed a bottle of sauvignon blanc or pinot gris—it's going to go great with your cheese selection.

Goat Cheese, Chicken, and Goji Wrap

This isn't really a recipe; it's more of a creative inspiration from Mt. Lehman Cheese Co. for a tasty little snack and a great way to explore Jason Dykstra's beautiful cheese combined with fresh goji berries from Gojoy (page 59) in Langley.

Serves 2

6 Tbsp Mt. Lehman Cheese herb and garlic chèvre

2 sun-dried tomato soft tortillas

½ cup grated Mt. Lehman Cheese Matsqui aged goat cheddar

1 cup Gojoy goji berries (blueberries also work well)

1 cooked, seasoned chicken breast, cooled and chopped

1. Spread about 3 Tbsp chèvre on each tortilla. Sprinkle with the cheddar, some of the goji berries, and the chicken. Roll into a log, cut in half, and enjoy!

Field House Brewing

2281 W. Railway St., Abbotsford, V2S 2E3; 604-776-2739
fieldhousebrewing.com

It is an exciting time for craft beer fans: they finally have choices! And craft beer in Abbotsford is a booming industry. Field House Brewing is an excellent place to indulge in some high-quality craft beer in a high-quality environment. Not only is the beer great, but the whole experience of visiting Field House is incredible. Located within a stone's throw of the historic downtown core of old Abbotsford, you recognize immediately that something is different; the vibe is smooth, hip, and very Vancouver-esque. They have definitely found their brewing mojo, and their customers are obviously loving it!

Attached to the Field House brewery is a cozy tasting room with a great wood-burning fireplace, but it is their outdoor space that really impresses. Their 3,000-square-foot front yard, or "beer lawn" as they call it, is licensed, so you can spread out a blanket or pull up a table. There are families with kids drinking craft sodas and snacking on food from local food trucks. There is bocce and horseshoes, live music, and card games—sometimes even yoga! It feels like hanging out in your best friends' backyard, only they have 10 beers on tap in their living room, including a guest tap and a local cider! It's hard to imagine ever leaving.

Field House is all about local. The wine they sell is from Mt. Lehman (page 118), the food and snacks they sell are from local producers, and they work closely with Chef Bonnie Friesen (page 195) from Faspa and Company to create delicious food and beer pairing events. My current favorite is the radler—a seasonal rotator of a mixture of beer and juice. Traditionally it is grapefruit juice mixed with a lager or wheat beer, but the flavors and profiles at Field House change at the whim of the brewmaster, and I, for one, appreciate the whimsy! The staff at the bar are knowledgeable and eager to tell you how the beer is made and how they incorporate as many local ingredients as possible. When you're in Abbotsford, this is a must-visit.

A guest tap at a brewery is a way for the brewer to sort of show off or highlight something they like that another brewery is doing that maybe they themselves aren't. Sometimes a guest tap isn't even a beer; it can be a cider or a root beer. Giving up one of the taps in a craft brewery to a competitor is a huge compliment. You should always give it a taste!

Nature's Pickin's Market

1356 Sumas Way, Abbotsford, V2S 8R2; 604-855-3374
naturespickins.ca

Caroline and Doug Phillips own Nature's Pickin's Market in Abbotsford and they are some of the nicest people you will ever meet. Their store is beautiful and obviously run by people who take tremendous pride in what they do. Nature's Pickin's works directly with local farmers to bring their products to market—and with neighbors like Birchwood Dairy (page 127), Gelderman Farms (page 129), Taves Family Farms (page 131), and Willow View Farms, they have top-quality choices. When Nature's Pickin's opened their doors in the summer of 2000, the Phillipses' dream was to bring local farmers' bounty of fresh fruit and vegetables to a farmers-style market that was available year-round. Although they do sell some imported goods as well, selling local is their first priority. If you find yourself in Abbotsford running short on time, you can always stock up on a ton of great local items by just stopping here.

Set against the stunning backdrop of Mt. Baker, Nature's Pickin's Market is in the middle of a not-so-ordinary farm. The farm it is located on is also home to the EcoDairy in partnership with Science World, where, they say, they are "inspiring young minds to discover the science and technology behind where their food comes from." The EcoDairy is a demonstration farm where, with the help of mascot Vicki the Cow, you'll learn everything you ever wanted to know about dairy cows and probably some stuff you didn't want to know (ecodairy.ca).

Behind Nature's Pickin's, beyond the blueberry and blackberry fields, you'll find a rice paddy. That's right, a rice paddy in Abbotsford! The rice is harvested for Canada's first locally produced fresh premium sake. The small-batch production is made from

100 percent BC-grown rice—a dream come true for the Artisan Sake Maker in their passionate pursuit to produce a truly Canadian sake (artisansakemaker.com).

Outside the market, you can't miss the bleating of the goats on the roof as they keep the grass growing there nice and trimmed. Springtime on the farm is so exciting with the birth of all the baby animals, and below the goats you have the pleasure of meeting all of the other farm animals: Dora the donkey, Angel and the other mini horses, the baby calves, and last but not least, the pigs and turkeys. It's a great free experience for little ones and the not-so-little ones in the family.

Life on the farm for Nature's Pickin's Market goes beyond what is harvested in the fields, whether it is the no-spray U-pick blueberries or the hundreds of pounds of fresh produce. It's about people, businesses, and farmers with a vision for education, sustainability, and supporting their local community.

Local farmers rely on Nature's Pickin's to help them sell some volume! One of the consistently best-selling items in the market is potatoes. Fresh potatoes are delivered by the truckload every week. They come from Heppell's Potato Corporation in Surrey, and they're well priced and absolutely fly out of the market along with all of the other weekly features. I would be remiss if I didn't remind you to check the deli case, refrigerator, and freezer for the Fireside Kitchen entrées, sides, and soups—you'll want to stock up!

Potato Pepper Chowder

Caroline Phillips *loves* to cook. Her passion for all things local is really evident in this simple yet delicious chowder. She recommends enjoying this dish with fresh sourdough bread and lots of butter!

Serves 4

6 slices bacon, diced

2 Tbsp unsalted butter

1 medium yellow onion, diced

1 leek, diced

2 stalks celery, diced

3 medium red potatoes, peeled and diced

2 red bell peppers, diced

⅓ cup all-purpose flour

5 cups chicken stock

1 bay leaf

1 tsp chopped thyme leaves

Salt and pepper

1 large carrot, grated

1 cup whipping cream

1. In a frying pan over medium-high heat, cook the diced bacon until well cooked but not too crispy. Remove the bacon from the pan and set aside, leaving the fat in the pan. Turn down the heat to medium. Add the butter to the residual fat, then add the onions, leeks, celery, potatoes, and peppers in that order. Stir to combine and cook until tender, about 7 minutes.

2. Add the flour and stir to incorporate it into the fat. Slowly pour in the chicken stock, stirring until smooth. Add the bay leaf, thyme, salt and pepper to taste, the grated carrots, and the cooked bacon. Turn down the heat and simmer, uncovered, for 45 minutes, stirring occasionally.

3. Add the whipping cream and continue to simmer on low heat for another 15 minutes, stirring occasionally. Taste and season with more salt and pepper if necessary.

4. This soup can be left chunky or blended for a few seconds to make it extra creamy.

Maan Farms

790 McKenzie Rd., Abbotsford, V2S 7N4; 604-864-5723
maanfarms.com

When planning your trip to Maan Farms, give yourself plenty of time to experience everything they have to offer. There's so much to see and do—entire days could disappear before you knew what happened. And if you're looking for a sure-fire way to play out the kids, this is it—you will definitely have a peaceful drive home when everyone in your back seat is passed out!

At Maan Farms, you will find a fresh farm market bursting with peak-of-the-season produce, a bistro, a winery where they make wines from grapes and other fruit grown on the farm, a giant inflatable bouncy pillow, a petting zoo, a zip line, a pedal go-cart track, a corn maze, a playground, face painting, and crafts! You can pick your own berries when they're in season or buy them already picked. If you have never had the pleasure of picking your own berries, you should give it a go. Somehow they just taste a bit better when you've had to work for them. While the kids are playing themselves out, you can hit the winery and sample one of their delicious wines. Their merlot, cabernet sauvignon, and cabernet franc are enticing and will make a great addition to your dinner table or picnic basket, but they're better known for their fruit wines, which sell out year after year. Table wines and dessert wines made from their own strawberries, blueberries, blackberries, and raspberries are perfect patio sippers or terrific turned into a fresh fruit sangria. The dessert wines pair perfectly with dark chocolate or a rich creamy cheesecake. My mouth waters just remembering the intense juicy flavors from their Raspberry Dessert Wine—it is phenomenal. The wines vary according to the seasons, so check the website before you go to see what's available—but know that it will be good regardless of what fruit has been used.

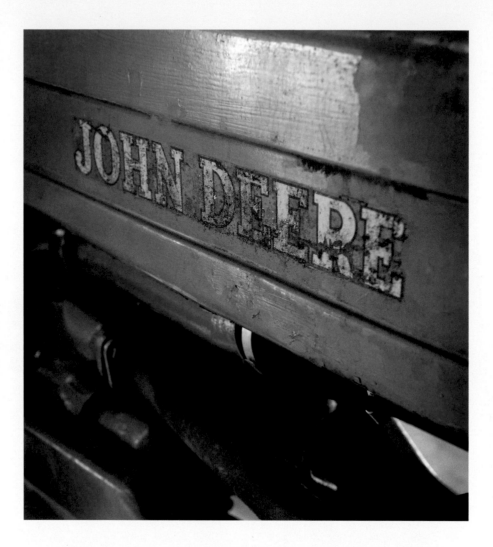

Over the years, Maan Farms has always been known for their delicious strawberries, raspberries, and blueberries. When Grandma and Grandpa Maan opened their first roadside stand in 1982, they were selling what quickly became known as "the juiciest strawberries in the Fraser Valley." As their reputation grew, so did their business. Today, Kris and Devinder Maan, the second generation of farmers, are assisted by the third generation, Preena, Gurleen, Gaurav, and Amir—the whole family is involved. You can tell from the environment and the produce at the farm that they love what they do. You don't get results that tasty without putting lots of love into it.

Fruit Wine and Summer Berry Sangria

Sangria is a great addition to just about any summer BBQ or patio party. My recipe for it is a good one to get you started if you haven't made it before (or even if you have, of course). Once you have the basic ratio down, you can change it up with any ripe berries and your favorite wines.

Makes about 8 standard glasses

1 cup sliced strawberries

1 cup raspberries

1 cup blackberries

1 bottle (750 mL) Maan Farms fruit table wine (the Strawberry/Raspberry Blend is excellent)

1 cup Maan Farms Raspberry Dessert Wine

Ice cubes

Club soda, chilled

Mint and sliced oranges or lemons, for garnish

1. In a large pitcher, combine the berries with the wines and stir to combine. Refrigerate for 2 hours or overnight. The longer you leave the fruit in the wine, the softer it will get, so it's up to you, really.

2. When you're ready to serve, fill some tall glasses with plenty of ice. Pour the sangria three-quarters of the way full and top with club soda. Stir to combine. Garnish with a fresh mint sprig and a slice of orange or lemon and serve immediately.

Chef Dez

Can be found at: Various locations throughout the Valley
(look for his column in local newspapers).
chefdez.com

You've probably never met anyone quite as enthusiastic about cooking and sharing their passion for good food as Chef Dez. Chef Dez, aka Gordon Desormeaux, is a best-selling cookbook author, a chef, a columnist, a brand manager for the Big Green Egg BBQ, and a dad and a husband based in Abbotsford. Chef Dez gave up restaurant life to teach people to make better food at home and, for many years, taught classes at local cooking schools, public schools, and community events. Dez learned to cook as a young boy; his mom spent hours with him in the kitchen teaching him to make everything from stocks and sauces to baked goods. At the age of 13, little Gordon presented his family with his first gourmet meal—duck à l'orange. Can you imagine?! This was long before the Food Network, so Dez was obviously born with a flair for the delicious. Food doesn't have to be complicated or fancy to be tasty, but you do need to have a little finesse, some patience, and good ingredients—and hey, take a minute or two to present it well! As Chef Dez says, "You eat with your eyes first. A little garnish never killed anyone!"

At his cooking classes and demonstrations, Chef Dez always has plenty of opportunities to highlight local ingredients and producers. Cooking seasonally with some inspiration from the Mediterranean, the Deep South, or Mexico, Dez encouraged his students to recreate in their own homes the recipes he shared, and he provided them with the skills and confidence to put better food on their tables more often.

When you read one of Chef Dez's columns, published regularly in some of the Fraser Valley newspapers, take part in one of his classes, or watch him on a cooking stage at a local event, you'll always take away a few great tips and tricks for putting great food on your table too!

Fire-Roasted Corn and Black Bean Salsa

Try this for a fantastic accompaniment at your next BBQ. It's great on grilled steak, chicken, and fish. Or serve it as an appetizer alongside your favorite tortilla chips.

Makes about 4 cups

2 cobs sweet corn, husks removed

1 large red bell pepper, in large pieces

1 medium red onion, in thick rounds

2 Tbsp vegetable oil

½ cup canned black beans, rinsed and drained

¼ cup soft sun-dried tomatoes, finely chopped

¼ cup firmly packed finely chopped cilantro

2 cloves garlic, minced

Zest of 1 lime, finely chopped

Juice of 1 lime

½ tsp salt

¼ tsp pepper

1. Preheat your grill to 450°F.

2. Using a silicone brush, brush the corn, bell peppers, and onions with the oil. Put them directly on the hot grill and cook, turning often, until you have nice char marks and the vegetables are starting to soften, about 12 minutes. Remove from the grill and place them on a plate to cool completely.

3. Using a sharp knife, remove the corn from the cobs, then discard the cobs. Place the kernels in a medium-size bowl. Cut the red pepper pieces into small dice and place them in the bowl with the corn.

4. Stir in the remaining ingredients, toss, and serve. The fresh salsa will keep in a sealed container in the refrigerator for up to 3 days.

The Big Dog Burger (recipe on page 154)

Chef Kevin Legge

Can be found at: BBQ competitions all over the world
www.bbqdog.ca

Kevin Legge is the head cook and pitmaster for Big
Dog BBQ, a competition BBQ team. You can find
Kevin, his teammate, John Baker, and Kevin's wife,
Colleen, competing in the professional BBQ circuit all
over BC, including the Barn Burner BBQ hosted at
the Fraser Valley Specialty Poultry Farm Store (page 181)
in April in Chilliwack's Yarrow neighborhood.

In 2014, Team Big Dog made a burger as part of
the competition at one of the local BBQ contests.
They tweaked it and labored over it for months leading up to the competition. The
Big Dog championship burger won that competition, and part of their prize was an
invitation to compete at the World Food Championships in Las Vegas. Kevin and
John spent the fall perfecting their recipe in preparation for some very intense
competition in Vegas. They packed their suitcases with their secret seasonings, knives,
and bravado, and boarded that plane! Two days of intense competition left Team Big
Dog with a second-place finish in the "signature burger" category. Kevin and John
had won second place at the World Food Championships, meaning they'd made the
second-best burger in the WORLD! The Big Dog Burger is now their signature burger.

Kevin, John, and Colleen continue to compete and to experiment with new
burger combinations. Kevin credits his success to his relationship with his butcher,
Carlo Bonetti at Bonetti Meats (page 70), who always supplies him with the
best-quality meat he can get.

Kevin and John aren't professional chefs; they're very accomplished home cooks who
love to BBQ, Southern style—low and slow, over charcoal and wood, the way it's supposed
to be done. They can be found almost every weekend, rain or shine, smoking something!

The Big Dog Burger

This is how Kevin Legge and John Baker build the signature Big Dog Burger that won them second place at the 2014 World Food Championships in Vegas. Kevin prefers to use fresh meat from Bonetti Meats for his Big Dog Burger. Carlo Bonetti (page 70) grinds it fresh to Kevin's specifications: a blend of 70 percent AAA beef chuck roast that is nicely marbled and 30 percent boneless pork shoulder. (Recipe photo on page 152)

Makes 6 burgers

Frizzled Onion Crisps
2 large sweet onions

1 cup buttermilk

Enough vegetable oil to deep-fry the onions (you need at least 4 inches in a medium-size saucepan)

1 cup all-purpose flour

1 tsp salt

1 tsp pepper

¼ tsp sweet Spanish paprika

The Buns
6 fresh hamburger buns

Garlic Aioli
1 cup full-fat mayonnaise

3 whole heads roasted garlic (see sidebar)

¼ cup lemon juice (1–2 lemons)

2 Tbsp grated parmesan

1½ tsp Dijon mustard

⅛ tsp cayenne pepper

Dash of Worcestershire sauce

3 Tbsp finely chopped flat-leaf parsley

Salt and pepper

The Meat and Cheese
3 lb ground meat pressed into ½ lb patties

Steak spice

12 slices Bonetti's thick-cut, double-smoked bacon

6 slices smoked gouda

The Veggies
2 garden-fresh ripe beefsteak tomatoes, in 6 thick slices

12 large basil leaves

12 thick-cut, cross-sliced bread-and-butter pickles

1. For the onion crisps, slice the onions very thin. If you have a mandoline, this would be a great time to use it. In a medium-size bowl, soak the sliced onions in the buttermilk, stirring to make sure they're completely covered, for about 30 minutes.

2. While the onions soak, prepare the aioli. To a small food processor or blender, add all of the aioli ingredients and process until smooth. Transfer to a small container with a tight-fitting lid. Leftover aioli will keep refrigerated for up to 7 days.

3. Preheat your grill to about 400°F. Kevin and John cook their burgers over charcoal on an old-fashioned Weber Kettle BBQ, but a gas grill or a cast iron grill pan will also work.

4. For the meat, season each patty generously on the outside with your favorite steak spice, then grill the patties until cooked through, about 14 minutes or until a digital meat thermometer inserted into the center of a patty reaches 170°F.

5. Lightly toast the buns and cook the bacon while the patties cook.

6. Right before the burgers are ready to come off the grill, top them each with a slice of cheese and allow it to start to melt. Remove the patties from the grill and put them on a platter to rest while you cook the onion crisps and prepare your buns.

7. After the onion slices have soaked for 30 minutes, in a medium-size saucepan over high heat, heat the vegetable oil to 375°F. You should use a deep-fry thermometer to ensure your oil is hot enough. If the oil isn't hot enough, the onions will be greasy and soggy—and that is not an awesome topping for any burger! While your oil is heating, in a medium-size bowl, combine the flour, salt, pepper, and paprika. Stir to evenly combine.

8. Remove one small handful of the onions at a time from the buttermilk and shake off the excess milk. Drop the onions into the seasoned flour mixture, tossing with a fork to make sure all the onions are coated. Remove from the flour, shaking again to remove the excess flour, and drop them into the hot oil. Deep-fry, stirring occasionally, until the onions are crispy and golden brown, about 4 minutes. Remove from the oil with a slotted spoon and drain on a paper towel. Season immediately with a pinch of salt.

9. Slather each side of the toasted buns with garlic aioli. Transfer a burger patty to the bottom half of each bun. Top each burger with two slices of bacon, a slice of tomato, two fresh basil leaves, two pickles, and a pile of the frizzled onion crisps. Finally, put the top half of the bun on and serve immediately with plenty of napkins!

⇛⟭

How to Roast Garlic

With a very sharp knife, cut the top off the whole head of garlic, just enough to slightly expose the cloves. Place in a small baking dish and drizzle with 1 tsp olive oil. Cover with aluminum foil. Bake at 400°F for about 30 minutes, or until the cloves are slightly golden brown and feel soft when pressed. Remove from the oven, remove the foil, and cool. When you can handle the whole heads, gently squeeze the roasted garlic into a small bowl.

⇛⟭

Chef Jeff Massey

Can be found at: Restaurant 62, 33559 Marshall Rd., Abbotsford, V2S 3N5;
604-855-3545
restaurant62.ca

Chef Jeff Massey left the fast-paced life of a Yaletown chef to pursue his culinary passion in the Fraser Valley in the early 2000s. Jeff's philosophy has always been to create and maintain a menu featuring locally inspired, ingredient-driven, and most importantly, simple and delicious food. He is definitely succeeding!

Inspired by the flavors of the Mediterranean, Restaurant 62 is well known for its innovative regional menu, award-winning wine selection, comfortable ambience, and impeccable service. Just north of Highway 1 on McCallum Road, Restaurant 62 is easy to find and has become known as *the* destination for fine local cuisine in the Fraser Valley. For more than 10 years, Chef Jeff and the team at R62, as it's known locally, have worked hard to honor their commitment to support local, organic food and producers. If you're there for lunch, chances are pretty good you will see a local farmer saunter in, carrying his wares for the kitchen. He'll be greeted with a firm handshake or a hug and always afforded a few minutes to chat. Using as much local product as possible means the menu changes often—but it always has a fantastic array of fresh seasonal food on offer. So if you haven't been to Restaurant 62 for a long time, perhaps you're due for another visit. If you've never been, it should definitely be on your to-do list. And on your way to the table, give Chef Jeff a wave. You'll see him and the R62 team in action in their open kitchen. (It's always fun to sneak a peek at what they're plating up, and it might help you decide what to order.)

Photo opposite: Seared Fraser Valley Chicken
(recipe on page 158)

Seared Fraser Valley Chicken Breast with Farmhouse Alpine Gold Polenta

I'm always happy to see polenta on the menu at Restaurant 62. I wish it was on more menus and used in more recipes. Hopefully this recipe from Chef Jeff will encourage you to make it at home and cook with it more often. It's really delicious! (Recipe photo on page 156)

Serves 4

Chicken Breasts
¼ cup duck fat

4 Fraser Valley boneless, skin-on chicken breasts

Soft Alpine Gold Polenta
2 Tbsp olive oil

1 tsp minced shallots

½ tsp minced garlic

½ tsp sambal oelek

½ cup dry white wine (see sidebar)

2 cups chicken stock

1 cup whole milk

1 cup cornmeal

1 cup grated Farm House Natural Cheeses Alpine Gold cheese

Salt and pepper

1. Preheat the oven to 400°F.

2. For the chicken, heat a large ovenproof frying pan over medium-high heat, then add the duck fat to liquefy. Sear the chicken breasts, skin side down, until golden brown and crispy. Turn them over, then transfer the pan to the oven for about 12 minutes or until cooked through. The chicken should have an internal temperature of about 175°F.

3. For the polenta, in a large heavy-bottomed saucepan, warm the olive oil over medium heat, then add the shallots, garlic, and sambal oelek. Stirring constantly, sweat the shallots and garlic, being careful not to let them brown. Once they are translucent, deglaze the pan with the white wine, scraping the tasty bits off the bottom. Add the chicken stock and milk, increase the heat to medium-high, and bring to a simmer. Once the mixture is at a simmer, whisk in the cornmeal. Switch to a spatula or wooden spoon and cook for about 10 minutes, stirring constantly. If the polenta is boiling too vigorously or sticking to the pot, turn down the heat to low. As the polenta starts to thicken, add the cheese and continue to stir. Once thick, yet still creamy, season to taste. Remove from the heat and serve immediately with the cooked chicken breasts.

When you're cooking with wine, please cook only with wine you would drink. The "cooking wine" you buy at the supermarket is terrible and loaded with salt and preservatives. When you open a bottle of wine to cook with, be sure to taste it first to check its quality— I'm sure you're familiar with the saying "a little for the pot, a little for the cook," so pour a glass and enjoy it while you cook.

Chef Tracy Dueck

Can be found at: Tracycakes, #101 2636 Montrose Ave., Abbotsford, V2S 3T6;
604-852-1904, and
21594 — 48th Ave, Langley, V3A 3M5; 604-427-1424
tracycakesonline.com

In 2006, Tracy Dueck opened Tracycakes Bakery Café. I'm sure some of you will remember the cupcake craze of 2007 and 2008. That was partially Tracy's fault! They were so delicious; how could anyone resist? Tracy opened this first café to serve wholesome homemade meals, high tea, and freshly baked cupcakes with real buttercream icing, just like she fed her own family. The idea of treating her customers like family stayed with Tracy as her business grew, and now her family—daughters Melissa and Jessica—work with her in the business to share the values their mom and her mother before her taught them. Tracy and her daughters are lovely, charming, and pretty—just like the cafés and the cupcakes.

The interior of the cafés is a fancy sort of shabby chic. Tracy is a DIY kinda girl, so there are bits and pieces of her whimsical creativeness all over the place. Mismatched chairs, tea in real teacups, and a cupcake showcase that will make even those with the strongest willpower drool! Every day, Tracy and her team serve soup, sandwiches, a proper high tea, sweets, and lots of her signature cupcakes to enjoy in the cafés or to go. And whenever possible, Tracy incorporates local ingredients into her recipes.

Although the cupcake craze of 2008 came to an end (slowly, but it did eventually end), Tracycakes stood the test of time because they weren't just a fad. They're delicious, and a Tracycakes cupcake will always put a smile on anyone's face—that is never going away. Tracy and her team make about 60 varieties of cupcakes and babycakes (minis) on a rotating basis—Almond Joy, Gingerbread, Ra Ra Raspberry,

Jamaican Me Crazy, Lemon, German Chocolate, and Mango & Lavender, just to name a few. You can preorder a full-size cake or cupcakes for any occasion, and wedding cakes are a weekly occurrence for Tracy and her team.

You can call ahead and get a lunch to go to take on your travels as a picnic, but if you have the time and can plan a leisurely late-morning/early afternoon visit with a friend, call and book high tea. It is so civilized! Dainty finger sandwiches, mini quiches, Tracy's homemade scones with clotted cream and jam, sliced fruit, sweets, and babycakes on an old-fashioned three-tiered tea tray make every visit feel special. Pinkies up!

Tracycake Scones
(recipe on page 163)

Never-Fail Pastry (and it never fails!)

Easy as pie? Not always. Good pastry is hard! It can be tricky and finicky until you find your mojo. This recipe from Tracy is your new mojo. We all need more pie in our lives, and this recipe will indeed make it easy.

Makes enough for 1 (9-inch) double-crust pie

2 cups all-purpose flour

¾ tsp salt

1 cup shortening, at room temperature

1 egg

2 Tbsp cold water

1 Tbsp white vinegar

1. Combine the flour and salt in a mixing bowl. Cut the shortening into the flour with a pastry blender or two knives until the mixture resembles coarse crumbs.

2. In a separate bowl, beat the egg, water, and vinegar together to blend. Pour this over the flour mixture. Stir with a fork until the mixture is evenly moistened.

3. Divide the dough in half and shape each half into a ball. Flatten each ball into a circle about 4 inches in diameter. Wrap and chill the dough for about 15 minutes for easier rolling.

4. Dust a rolling pin and work surface lightly with flour. Roll out each piece of dough separately until it is a uniform thickness and about 10 inches in diameter. If the dough sticks, dust it lightly with flour.

5. Ease one piece of the pastry into the pie plate without stretching. After filling the pie, repeat with the remaining piece of pastry for a top crust (or use it for a second pie). Trim, flute, and bake according to your filling recipe.

Pie crust can be made and frozen for future use, but it isn't ideal to do this. Freezing expands and contracts the water in pie crust, which tends to break down its structure, leaving you with a finished product that is usually less flaky. Make what you need, when you need it. This recipe makes it too easy not to!

Bumbleberry Pie

Bumbleberry usually refers to a combination of any three types of berries, but Tracy will always encourage you to feel free to mix up her recipe a little if the raspberries and blueberries aren't ready at the same time!

Makes one (9-inch) pie
(serves 8)

1 cup + ¼–½ tsp sugar

⅓ cup cornstarch

2 cups blueberries

1 cup blackberries

1 cup raspberries

1 recipe Never-Fail Pastry
(page 161)

1. In a large bowl, combine the 1 cup sugar with the cornstarch. Add the blueberries, blackberries, and raspberries. Toss to combine.

2. Preheat the oven to 400°F.

3. While the oven is preheating, prepare a full recipe of Never-Fail Pastry and line a 9-inch pie dish with half of it. Place the filling in the pie shell. Dampen the crust edge and cover with the top pastry. Trim and crimp to seal. Pierce with a fork to vent. Sprinkle with the remaining sugar.

4. Place the prepared pie on a rimmed baking sheet (in case the fruit is extra juicy and bubbles over a little) and bake for 15 minutes. Turn down the heat to 350°F and continue to bake for another 40 minutes, until the pastry is golden and the filling is bubbly. Cool and serve.

Fresh Strawberries with Tracycake Scones

In the cafés, Tracy serves a lot of guests her traditional high tea, and a high tea would not be complete without a proper scone. Tracy's basic scone recipe is easily transformed into a delicious vessel to deliver fresh berries but is equally delicious with clotted cream and jam. (Recipe photo on page 160)

Makes about 1 dozen scones

Scones
1¾ cups all-purpose flour

⅓ cup sugar

2 tsp baking powder

½ tsp salt

½ cup cold unsalted butter, cubed

2 eggs

⅓ cup whole milk

Whipped cream and icing sugar, for serving

Strawberries
3 cups sliced strawberries

⅓ cup sugar (or as needed)

1 Tbsp lemon juice

1. Preheat the oven to 350°F. Line a baking sheet with parchment paper.

2. For the scones, in a food processor, place the flour, sugar, baking powder, salt, and butter, in this order. Pulse until it resembles a crumbly mix. Add the eggs and milk and pulse five to six times, until the dough comes together. Dust the counter with flour and turn out the dough. Knead a few times and roll out to about ½ inch thick.

3. With a 3-inch round cookie cutter, cut out scones and place them on the prepared baking sheet.

4. Bake for 10 to 12 minutes, or until golden brown. Do not overbake. Allow to cool while you prepare the strawberries.

5. Toss the strawberries with the sugar and lemon juice in a bowl. Top the freshly baked scones with the strawberry mixture, add a dollop of whipped cream, and dust the top with icing sugar. Serve and enjoy!

6. Leftover unfilled scones keep well in an airtight bag for up to 3 days or frozen for up to 1 month.

If you don't have fresh strawberries on hand, try serving with any mixed fresh berries instead.

Other Places to Visit

Bloom, The Abbotsford Tulip Festival

36737 North Parallel Rd., Abbotsford, V3G 2H5

Bloom is easily one of Canada's most beautiful festivals, featuring acre after acre of the most colorful tulip fields you will ever see, with more than 40 varieties of tulips on display. There's also a U-pick field, covered picnic tables, and a kids' play area. The festival runs through most of April and May, but because of the seasonality of the event, start days are flexible. Visit the website for dates and times before you venture out. (abbotsfordtulipfestival.ca)

Bhav's Indian Cuisine and Sweet Shop

2591 Cedar Park Pl., Abbotsford, V2T 3S4; 604-557-9492

Bhav's serves really good traditional Indian food that can be enjoyed by everyone. They ask you how spicy you like it before they make it, then adjust it accordingly. If ever there was a place to describe as "a hole in the wall," this is it. It's a great discovery. Never had Indian food before? No problem. Start with the butter chicken and naan bread— they're so incredibly delicious, you'll be hooked for sure! They don't have a website, so call or just drop by.

Duft and Co. Bakehouse

2636 Montrose Ave., Abbotsford, V2S 3T6; 604-744-2443

Tyler Duft and Cassandra Crocco make great food: perfect pastries, fresh sandwiches, homemade soup, and the lemon buns . . . good god, the lemon buns! (duftandco.com)

Lepp Farm Market

33955 Clayburn Rd., Abbotsford, V2S 7Z1; 604-851-5377

So much more than a grocery store! Fresh local produce, local meat, a deli, an in-store bakery, and the Farmers Table Café all prominently feature the food the Lepp family raises and farms. They host regular cooking classes and a corn festival that celebrates the harvest. Lepp Farm Market is a great place to stock up on local ingredients. (leppfarmmarket.com)

Oldhand Coffee

2617 Pauline St., Abbotsford, V2S 3S2; 778-779-3111

The coffee culture is alive and well in Abbotsford. This is a fantastic place to take a break from your day and enjoy warm hospitality, phenomenal coffee, superb pastries, and freshly made donuts. Oh, and for later in the day, they are licensed and make killer nachos! (oldhandcoffee.com)

Seaside Pearl Farmgate Winery

5290 Olund Rd., Abbotsford, V4X 1V6; 778-856-1312

Seaside Pearl is a relative newcomer to the winery scene in Abbotsford but their wine is already attracting a lot of attention. Their tasting room is a lovely little chapel with sweeping vistas of Mt. Lehman, perfectly suited to the farm setting. (seasidepearlwinery.ca)

Singletree Winery

5782 Mount Lehman Rd., Abbotsford, V4X 1V4; 604-381-1788

Since 2010, the Etsell family at Singletree Winery has been making some lovely wines. Of particular note are their aromatic whites like Siegerrebe, Grüner Veltliner, and a late harvest Kerner. This place is definitely worth a visit—be sure to check their website for tasting room hours so you aren't disappointed. (singletreewinery.com)

Tanglebank Gardens and Brambles Bistro

29985 Downes Rd., Abbotsford, V4X 1Z8; 604-856-9339

Tanglebank is a boutique nursery full of seasonal indoor and outdoor gardening inspiration. However, for me, keeper of the black thumb, it's the fantastic food in the bistro inside the nursery that's the key attraction. Go for brunch—the coffee is locally roasted and strong, the eggs are always perfectly cooked, and everything is made from scratch. It's truly excellent. (tanglebank.com)

Chilliwack

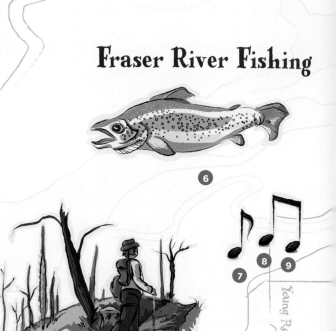

Fraser River Fishing

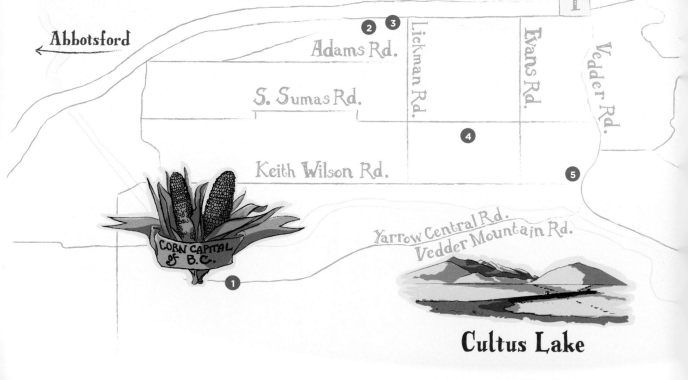

Abbotsford

Adams Rd.

S. Sumas Rd.

Keith Wilson Rd.

Lickman Rd.

Evans Rd.

Vedder Rd.

Young Rd.

Yarrow Central Rd.

Vedder Mountain Rd.

CORN CAPITAL of B.C.

Cultus Lake

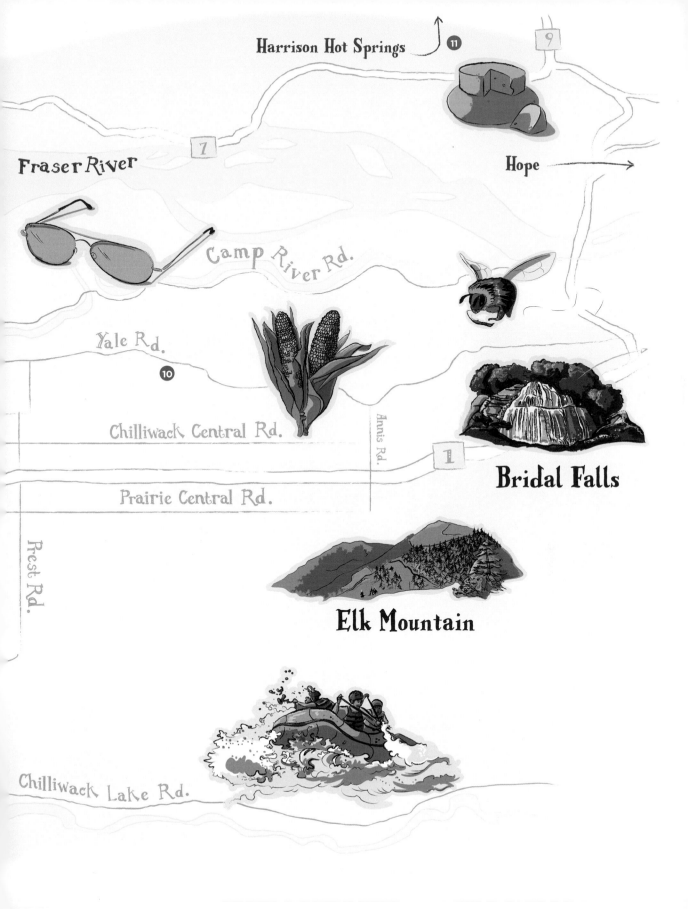

Chilliwack

Chilliwack is all about the outdoors. It is truly an adventurer's paradise. During your visit to Chilliwack, you can hike, bike, camp, fish for a giant sturgeon, play golf, water-ski, ride a horse, or go whitewater rafting. You can visit the farmgates, the museum, or a spa, or shop, eat, or sun yourself on a rock by the river or on a towel on the sand at the lake if you want a break from all the adrenaline. You can visit the scariest haunted house in BC, visit the Great Blue Heron Nature Reserve on the stunningly beautiful Vedder River floodplain, or simply sit and sip craft beer on a fabulous patio. The choices are endless.

Since 1873, when Chilliwack was incorporated and the main mode of transportation was a steamboat that transported people and goods up and down the Fraser River to New Westminster, the people of Chilliwack have embraced the riverfront lifestyle. With more than 80 parks covering about 350 acres in the region, the residents of Chilliwack take outdoor recreation very seriously!

When the almost 85,000 Chilliwackians who live in the area aren't recreating, they are farming. More than 900 working farms dot the landscape in Chilliwack, farming everything from goats to honeybees, corn, and berries. There is so much to enjoy in this region that you should plan your trip carefully or run the risk of encountering a million distractions—tasty, interesting distractions. (Hey, look, a chicken!) Getting "lost" intentionally in the area can also be a great strategy; just get in the car and drive. Sometimes being an accidental tourist, traveling without a plan or a destination in mind, can be fun, but for the planners in the crowd, you'll be spoiled for choice in the 'Wack. Chilliwack's neighboring communities, including Cultus Lake, Popkum, Yarrow, and Rosedale, offer even more places to explore.

No matter what time of year you visit, the seasonality of the region will shine, but my favorite time of year in the area is late summer and early fall. The Chilliwack corn is absolutely everywhere. Some might say it is the best-known crop in the region. Featured at drive-thru roadside stands and at markets, you really must buy it.

Chilliwack corn is famous for its quality, sweetness, and varieties of non-GMO cobs. There is truly nothing that compares to corn picked that morning, steamed that night, and served with a little (or a lot!) of local butter and salt.

Tourist information: tourismchilliwack.com
Facebook: @tourism_chilliwack
Instagram: @tourismchilliwack
Twitter: @greatoutside

Chilliwack is a must-visit for music lovers. The city has a thriving arts and culture community with a ton of choices in live music, from rock to the Chilliwack Symphony Orchestra, almost every weekend. In the height of summer, you can attend a variety of food-fueled events, including the Party in the Park on Friday nights in downtown Chilliwack—a night for the whole family featuring live music, face painting, food trucks, and beverages. Visit the Barn Burner BBQ Competition in Yarrow in April, a corn maze in August, and the Garlic and Rockabilly Music Festival in September.

What's that you say? You're not really an outdoors type of person? No problem! Chilliwack is also bursting with indoor options, with spas, museums, and shopping. You can always find a cozy café to grab a cup of tea or a hot bowl of soup if it's raining, or go see a show, a concert, or a play at the Chilliwack Cultural Centre. The Cultural Centre also has a great assortment of art classes for kids and adults alike. You do need to sign up in advance, but what a great excuse to plan your excursion.

The next time someone asks you what there is to do in the Fraser Valley, the answers will come easily!

The Local Harvest Market and Anita's Organic Mill

7697 Lickman Rd., Chilliwack, V2R 4A7; 604-846-6006
thelocalharvest.ca

A visit to the Local Harvest Market is really three stops in one. The Local Harvest Market sits on about 40 acres of prime Chilliwack farmland at the base of Vedder Mountain. They have a new, very modern market facility that includes Anita's Organic Mill (anitasorganic.com) retail outlet and the Market Bakery.

Anita's Organic Mill is a certified organic purveyor of grains, flours, and baking ingredients. At the Local Harvest Market, you can stock up on everything from dried cranberries to kamut flakes and Red Fife flour, both bagged and in bulk. If you're a baker, this place is ingredient heaven! But you don't have to be a baker to experience the delicious result of freshly milled grains. The Market Bakery transforms all of those organic ingredients from Anita's into bread and pizza baked in their wood-fired oven. The pizza is topped with veggies and a fresh tomato sauce made from tomatoes harvested just steps away from the bakery. The focaccia and sourdough breads will make you weep and leave you wishing you had a secret stash of fresh butter in the glove box for the ride home! The vision of sustainability underpinning the Local Harvest Market is evident in everything they do, but especially in the produce, which is sold the same day it is harvested.

When you visit, plan to spend an hour or two exploring outside of the store. You're welcome to take a walk around the farm, talk to the farm staff, and get a better understanding of how the farm works and why they do what they do. Or you can plan your visit around a workshop on cheesemaking or on preserving and canning, or a class like the Mushroom Identification Course, which teaches you to identify edible and poisonous mushrooms in the wild.

The motto at the Local Harvest Market is, "We go the extra mile so you don't have to." How awesome is that?

Sweet and Spicy Roasted Carrots with Parsnips and Chickpeas

Summer veggies are great, but I really think root veggies get a bum rap. The veggies at the Local Harvest Market are great all year, and with a little TLC (and pomegranate molasses), winter veggies can be as sexy as the spring ones—as you'll see from this recipe that they shared with me to share with you.

Serves 4 as a side

1 lb small carrots, peeled

½ lb parsnips, peeled

1 can (19 oz) chickpeas, drained and rinsed

3 Tbsp olive oil

1 tsp dried red chili flakes

½ tsp salt

2 Tbsp pomegranate molasses (see sidebar)

½ cup crumbled feta

2 Tbsp chopped flat-leaf parsley, for garnish

1. Preheat the oven to 400°F.

2. Halve the carrots and parsnips lengthwise. You want them roughly the same size. Transfer them to a rimmed baking pan and spread them out in a single layer. Add the chickpeas to the pan and drizzle everything with the oil. Sprinkle over the chili flakes and the salt and toss to combine. Place the pan in the hot oven and roast for 15 minutes.

3. Remove from the oven and turn over the veggies and stir the chickpeas to recoat with the oil. Return the pan to the oven and roast for another 15 minutes. Remove from the oven again. The veggies should be fork-tender and the chickpeas crispy.

4. Transfer to a platter to serve, drizzle the pomegranate molasses overtop, sprinkle the feta overtop, garnish with parsley, and serve warm.

Pomegranate molasses is available at specialty stores like Well Seasoned (page 107) and at Middle Eastern markets. It is pomegranate juice that has been reduced and turned into a syrup. It is intensely sour and is such a dark red it almost looks black. It adds incredible depth of flavor to sauces, vinaigrettes, dressings, and even cocktails. It is inexpensive and an ingredient you'll have fun playing with. Pick some up when you stop at Well Seasoned.

Chèvre–Stuffed Zucchini Pancakes

When they're in season, zucchini are abundant and inexpensive, but let's face it, how much can you really eat? I created this recipe to use up excess zucchini. It's perfect for a quick summer lunch or dinner on the deck. Chèvre from Milner Valley (page 37) takes it from tasty to awesome in just a few minutes.

Makes about 12 pancakes

1 lb small zucchini, grated and excess liquid squeezed out (see sidebar)

¼ cup grated yellow onion

1 Tbsp chopped basil

2 Tbsp chopped mint

2 tsp chopped lemon zest

½ tsp finely chopped garlic

1 tsp salt

½ tsp pepper

½ cup all-purpose flour

1 tsp baking powder

2 large eggs, beaten

½ cup olive oil

1 log (4 oz) Milner Valley chèvre, very thinly sliced

1. Preheat the oven to 200°F.

2. In a large bowl, combine the zucchini, onions, basil, mint, lemon zest, garlic, salt, and pepper. In a small bowl, combine the flour and baking powder. Add the eggs and the flour mixture to the vegetables and stir just until combined.

3. Heat a large nonstick frying pan over medium-high heat for 3 minutes. When hot, add enough of the oil to coat the bottom of the pan. Add the batter to the pan by tablespoons (making sure to spoon both batter and vegetables), leaving 1 inch between the cakes. Immediately drop a round of cheese into the center of each pancake. Top with another tablespoon of batter to enclose the cheese. Cook until golden brown on the bottom side, about 1 ½ minutes. Flip with a spatula and cook on the second side until crispy and golden brown, about 1 minute.

4. Remove from the pan and place on a baking sheet. Keep warm in the oven while preparing the remaining pancakes.

Grate your zucchini onto a clean tea towel. Roll the towel up and squeeze all the moisture from the zucchini, unroll the towel, redistribute the zucchini, and squeeze it again. Repeat until you have removed as much moisture from the zucchini as possible.

To cut chèvre, try using a piece of unflavored dental floss pulled tightly to slice thin disks of cheese from the log.

Happy Days Dairy—
Heavenly Cheese Deli

7350A Barrow Rd., Chilliwack, V1E 3H1; 604-823-7241
happydaysdairy.com

Happy Days Dairy is the largest pasteurizer of goat milk in western Canada, with a total of three processing plants and 12 farmers in BC and Alberta. All goat, all the time! The three plants—in Salmon Arm and Chilliwack, BC, and Ponoka, Alberta—are located near the family farms that provide the milk, ensuring the fresh milk is processed as soon as it arrives at each facility. At the Chilliwack location, you can visit the dairy to get a better understanding of the whole pasteurizing process and then sample the  finished product and shop at Heavenly Cheese Deli, where you can stock up on goat cheeses, goat milk, goat yogurt, goat butter, and even powdered goat milk.

Unless you're someone who has had to deal with lactose or dairy intolerances, I suppose it's hard to grasp how often milk or dairy is used in regular recipes. Powdered milk is great to have on hand for when you travel, for baking, or for that "oh my dog, there's no milk for my coffee" emergency. To make milk, simply mix 1 cup warm water with ¼ cup goat milk powder and voilà! If you bake with a pastry recipe that calls for buttermilk, try using goat milk—the lactic acid found in goat milk is the same as in buttermilk, yogurt, and sour cream, so goat milk will also produce a super-tender pastry.

Goat milk, in liquid and powder form, is also great for making soap. So when you find yourself with a little extra time on your hands and you're ready to channel your inner pioneer, you can find a ton of tutorials online and learn to whip up an artisan batch of goat soap, goat scrub, goat lip balm, or even goat lotion.

Chiles Rellenos con Mole de Avellana (Stuffed Poblanos with Hazelnut Mole)

Chef Rossana Ascencio combines her Mexican roots and appreciation for local food to turn a classic chiles rellenos recipe into an incredible way to highlight Happy Days goat cheese. Chiles rellenos is essentially stuffed peppers, but these stuffed peppers are finished with a mole sauce, Rossana's version of a traditional Mexican sauce made with ground chilies, nuts, and chocolate. The recipe is a bit labor intensive, but it's really worth the effort. Make a double batch of the mole. It freezes well and is particularly good heated up and served over roasted chicken with a nice rice pilaf.

Serves 4

Chiles Rellenos

⅓ cup diced yellow onions

2 cloves garlic, diced

2 Tbsp vegetable oil

Salt and pepper

3 ripe Roma tomatoes, puréed and strained

1 tart apple, peeled and diced

1 semi-ripe plantain, peeled and chopped

½ cup diced dried apricots

½ cup dark raisins

½ cup walnut pieces

½ cup sliced almonds

2 whole cloves

1 tsp dried Mexican oregano

1 tsp ground cinnamon

1½ lb Happy Days feta, crumbled (see sidebar on page 179)

4 fresh poblano chilies, tops, seeds, and veins removed (see sidebar on page 180)

Mole de Avellana

3 ripe Roma tomatoes

1 medium yellow onion, quartered

2 cloves garlic

1 Tbsp vegetable oil

2 dried mulato chilies (see sidebar on page 180)

4 dried pasilla chilies

1 dried ancho chili

½ tsp coriander seeds, toasted

¼ tsp anise seeds, toasted

1 ripe plantain, sliced into rounds, lightly fried, and reserved on paper towels

2 corn tortillas, lightly toasted, broken in pieces

1 cup hazelnuts, toasted

¼ stick cinnamon

½ tsp sugar

Salt

2 cups chicken or vegetable stock

⅓ cup chopped Mexican chocolate (60% cocoa or higher)

Garnish

¼ cup chopped hazelnuts, lightly roasted, skins rubbed off

1. For the chiles rellenos, in a large frying pan over medium heat, cook the onions and garlic in the oil until translucent. Season to taste with salt. Add the strained tomatoes, diced fresh and dried fruit, nuts, and spices. Season to taste with salt and pepper. Stir well to incorporate all the ingredients. Turn down the heat and simmer until all of the ingredients are soft and starting to melt together. Turn off the heat and stir in the crumbled feta.

2. With a paring knife, open a slit on the side of each poblano chili, and spoon the filling inside. Cover with aluminum foil and reserve in a warm place until ready to serve.

3. For the mole, in a dry frying pan over medium-high heat, fry the tomatoes, onions, and garlic, turning them often until the exteriors are evenly charred/slightly burnt and the interiors start to barely soften. With tongs, remove them from the pan and set aside.

4. Add the oil to a separate pan, place it over medium-high heat, and add the charred tomatoes, onions, and garlic. Leave these to sauté as you prepare the chilies.

5. Working on one dried chili at a time, use a paring knife to cut a slit all the way down one side. Open up the chili and remove the stem, seeds, and as much of the veins as you can. Heat a large frying pan over medium heat. Lay the chilies flat in the dry pan and just heat through to dry-roast them. You don't want to get any color on them; you're just bringing out some of the flavors. Turn them over a few times, and as soon as you start to smell them, take them off the heat.

6. Add all of the dry-roasted chilies to a small saucepan and barely cover them with water. Bring it to a boil over medium heat, then remove the pan from the heat. Let the chilies sit in the hot water to soften and plump up for about 10 minutes. They'll be nice and soft.

7. Remove the chilies from the boiling water, discarding the water, and add them to the pan with the vegetables. Add the coriander and anise seeds and then the plantain slices. Mix well. Add the corn tortillas, hazelnuts, cinnamon, and sugar. Season to taste with salt. Continue to cook over medium heat, stirring occasionally, until all the ingredients are well incorporated, about 5 minutes.

Instead of feta, use 1½ lb pork, ground beef, chicken. If you use these, add them to the pan once the onions and garlic are translucent, and fully cook, using a spoon to break up the meat, for about 15 minutes.

When you're working with chilies, you should wear disposable gloves and wash your hands thoroughly with soap and warm water after handling. No one needs to go blind making dinner!

8. Add the stock, bring to a boil, then turn the heat down to low and simmer for 10 to 15 minutes, stirring occasionally to incorporate all the ingredients. The vegetables and chilies should be soft and the mixture will look like a loose sauce.

9. Allow to cool slightly, remove and discard the cinnamon stick, then transfer the mixture to a blender or food processor and purée to a smooth consistency. If necessary, blend in batches, and add a little more stock or water to the blender if the mixture is too thick.

10. Once you have a smooth sauce, strain it into a lightly oiled hot saucepan over medium heat. Cook the sauce for about another 5 minutes, stirring occasionally to further reduce the liquid. It should have a thick enough consistency to coat the back of the spoon. If it gets too thick, add a bit more stock; if it's too thin, continue to cook to reduce it.

11. When the sauce has reached its desired consistency, turn the heat down to low and add the Mexican chocolate, stirring well to allow the chocolate to melt and incorporate into the sauce. Season to taste, and simmer gently until you're ready to serve.

12. To serve, place a spoonful of the mole in the center of each plate, place a stuffed poblano on top, and cover with another spoonful of the mole. Sprinkle the chopped hazelnuts on top to garnish.

The Farm Store at Fraser Valley Specialty Poultry

4540 Simmons Rd., Chilliwack, V2R 4R7; 604-798-9044
fvsp.com

Meet the Falks.

The Falk family runs Fraser Valley Specialty Poultry, a three-generation family duck and goose farm in Chilliwack, right at the base of Vedder Mountain in Yarrow. The Falk family has been farming there since the early 1970s, and their farm has truly become a local landmark. They raise ducks, geese, specialty and organic chickens, and squab for retail customers and some of the finest restaurants and specialty markets in the province. At the Farm Store, you can purchase a myriad of their value-added products, like duck sausage, smoked duck, "duckeroni" (like pepperoni but made with duck), duck smokies, duck confit, duck pot pie, duck chili . . . you get the idea! The Grade A Pekin duck is available fresh or frozen and is perfect for roasting or cooking on your BBQ. You can buy duck pieces and parts and have your choice of either Pekin or Muscovy duck breast. They also sell duck fat, which makes a killer confit or a must-have for *the* most delicious oven-roasted potatoes.

The Farm Store also carries a great assortment of other locally raised protein—beef, pork, and even seafood—along with a variety of other locally made products and tons of tasty treats from local bakeries and artisan cheesemakers. You can always get a cup of hot freshly brewed coffee or a cold drink inside. It's a great place to stop when you need a break from driving to stretch your legs and replenish your picnic basket.

People who love to cook will have a difficult time leaving empty-handed. The shelves are loaded with inspiration. Ready-made duck confit, sold in packages of two in the store, may be the ultimate in decadent convenience; duck pot pie, duck chili, and duck pâté are also available in the freezer. So don't forget to leave some room in your ice chest. You're going to have a hard time resisting the urge to take one of everything home with you.

In the spring, the Farm Store plays host to the Barn Burner BBQ, a fantastic free community event that draws competitive BBQ teams from all over the Pacific Northwest to compete in cooking chicken, ribs, pulled pork, and beef brisket. This BBQ competition is a great way for competition teams to show off the quality of our local meat. Visitors can sample for free, buy great food, and enjoy live music, face painting, and a climbing wall. It's definitely the tastiest day of the year in Yarrow! All of the information about the BBQ competition can be found at barnburnerbbq.ca.

Whole Roasted Fraser Valley Duck

For some reason, roasting a whole duck intimidates people, but the Falks' method makes it almost as easy as roasting a chicken or turkey. The process is similar, but you have to turn the bird over several times during the cooking process to crisp up the skin. A lot (I mean a lot) of fat renders from the duck while it's cooking, so it's really important it cooks on a rack in a roasting pan so it isn't sitting in the fat and juices. Every time I roast a duck, I wonder why I don't do it more often. Give it a try—seriously, it's easy! You carve it and serve it exactly the same way you would any other whole bird. Instead of a gravy, try serving it with homemade applesauce or one of the preserves from Vista D'oro (page 31).

Serves 4

1 (6 lb) whole fresh Pekin duck (see sidebar)
2 cups boiling water
1 Tbsp salt
1 tsp pepper

Pekin duck is also known as Long Island duck, a domestic descendant of the Mallard featuring a prominent yellow bill, white plumage, and orange webbed feet. "Peking duck" is often how a Pekin duck is prepared in a Chinese restaurant (which is delicious, by the way!).

1. Preheat the oven to 425°F.

2. Remove your fresh duck from the bag, remove and discard the neck, giblets, and liver, and rinse the cavity and exterior under cold water. Trim off the excess fat from around the neck area. If your duck still has its wing tips on, cut them off with poultry shears. With a fork or the tip of a knife, prick the skin all over the bird about 12 times to allow the fat from under the skin to render while it cooks.

3. Place the duck, breast side up, on a rack in a roasting pan and slowly pour the boiling water all over. Remove the duck from the pan and pat it dry, leaving the water in the bottom of the pan. Season the duck inside and out with salt and pepper and return it to the roasting rack, breast side up again.

4. Put the roasting pan in the hot oven and roast, uncovered, for 1 hour. Remove the pan from the oven and, using two sets of tongs, turn the bird over, draining any liquid from the cavity back into the pan, so it's now sitting breast side down on the rack. Return the pan to the oven and roast for another hour.

5. Remove the pan from the oven and turn the bird over one more time, breast side up, for another 20 minutes of cooking, then remove from the oven. The duck skin will be very brown and crisp. (If you want to check the doneness of the duck with a digital thermometer, the temperature of the meat at the thickest part of the thigh or breast should be 165°F.)

6. Remove the pan from the oven and allow the duck to rest on the rack for 5 minutes. Drain any additional fat and juices from the cavity back into the pan and transfer the bird to a cutting board to rest for another 10 minutes before carving. Discard the fat and liquid remaining in the roasting pan.

Old Yale Brewing

44550 South Sumas Rd., Chilliwack, V2R 5M3; 604-392-2011
oldyalebrewing.com

Chilliwackians (isn't that an awesome word?) proudly claim to have the best drinking water in Canada. I can't verify that, but I can tell you that no one knows how to turn that water into award-winning beer like Old Yale Brewing. Since 2000, Old Yale has been honing their craft—and clearly, they have nailed it! For years, they struggled to keep up with the ever-growing demand for the craft beer they made in their small start-up brewery. In the summer of 2016, they moved into a new facility where they were able to seriously expand production, quenching the insatiable thirst of beer lovers all over BC.

You can buy signature brews at the brewery, or sip on a flight in the tasting room. While they rotate a seasonal selection through the taps, they're probably best known for their intensely hoppy West Coast IPA. I love their Moon Dance Mango Wheat, a creamy, soft beer with a distinctive mango note that pairs beautifully with grilled seafood and is great for sipping in the afternoon sun on the patio after a few hours' yard work. Another of their bestsellers is the stout. In 2014, their Sasquatch Stout was named Canada's Beer of the Year at the Canadian Brewing Awards. That is huge recognition for a small craft brewery in Chilliwack, and it cemented their reputation as a serious player in the industry. Even if you aren't a typical stout lover, it's easy to appreciate the complexity of this brew, with notes of coffee and cocoa. Its rich sweetness lends itself well to braised beef, stews, and French onion soup, and it's a great addition to fall desserts like chocolate cake and caramel sauce, and even dessert cocktails like the Sasquatch Float (page 185). Take some stout home with you and keep it on hand for cooking through the fall and winter.

When you visit Old Yale, try them all. You're sure to find something that speaks to you.

The Sasquatch Float

This is not the float of your youth (I hope), but it is the float of your future! When I first mixed these two ingredients, I felt like I had come across the world's next great culinary combo—you know, like peanut butter and chocolate. This float is a fun summertime dessert or pre-bedtime treat on those long summer nights when it's just too hot to fall asleep.

Serves 1

1 scoop vanilla ice cream

1 cup whole milk

2 oz Kahlúa or similar

2 oz Old Yale Brewing Sasquatch Stout

1. Drop the scoop of ice cream into a large rocks glass. Add the milk and Kahlúa and top with the stout. Serve immediately.

Fantasy Farms

9423 Gibson Rd., Chilliwack, V2P 6H4; 604-792-8572
fantasyfarmsinc.ca

Gary and Lisa Moran's motto is "You're either green and growing or you're ripe and rotting." They want everyone who visits Fantasy Farms to leave with a better understanding of how farming works and where their food comes from. Over the years, the farm has evolved to become very event-centric. The couple believes that farmers have to be creative to survive. When food isn't coming out of the ground, you need to find other ways to earn your living.

The couple got hooked on cultivating garlic because they wanted to host a garlic festival in the Fraser Valley and thought they'd better grow some themselves. In 2010, Lisa planted her first garlic crop—a whopping, and kind of unmanageable, 18 varieties. The next year, she scaled back to the two most popular: Russian Red and Music. Peeled Russian Red garlic cloves are sticky and sweet, and the bulb has an unmistakable purple hue. It can withstand soggy winter soils better than any other variety, so it's the perfect choice for Chilliwack. But it's not for the impatient! It's planted in September or October and harvested the following July. Music garlic bulbs have really large cloves—some the size of a small plum—that are easy to peel. The parchment-type skin is white with a slight pink hue. Music garlic is super-popular because of its moderately strong flavor, and I'm sure Lisa likes it because it thrives in the Fraser Valley's sometimes stressful growing conditions.

Nothing beats the flavor of farm-fresh garlic. All of Lisa's garlic is sold on the farm and, of course, at the Garlic and Rockabilly Festival (see the website for more information), so you can stock up when you visit. Garlic is easy to store in a dry, dark spot and lasts for ages.

Farm-Fresh Garlic Lovers' Dip

Lisa uses garlic as much as she possibly can, but her favorite way to use it is in this dip recipe, which the family fondly refers to as Yucky Dip. She says it's always a huge hit at any event, but you better make sure everyone there is eating it! Caution: You must love the taste of garlic for this one! The number of cloves you use depends on how strong you want it.

Makes about 2 cups

6-8 large cloves garlic, crushed

2 cups sour cream or Greek yogurt

¾-1 cup finely crumbled feta

¼ cup finely grated parmesan

2 Tbsp olive oil

2 Tbsp dried basil or other dried herbs (I use Well Seasoned's Tuscan blend)

1. In a medium-size bowl, use a spatula to mix the garlic, sour cream, feta, and parmesan together. Add the olive oil and mix to combine. You may need to add more oil, depending on your desired consistency. (I recommend the consistency of a thick sour cream.)

2. Mix your dried herbs in well and place the dip in an airtight container in the refrigerator for at least 6 hours, allowing all of the flavors to come together. When you're ready to serve, remove from the refrigerator and stir again, then transfer to a serving dish and serve with your favorite dippers. (Warning: Salty potato chips with this dip are ridiculously addictive.)

If you have any leftover dip, spread it on roasted potatoes 10 minutes prior to finishing, or slather it on raw chicken breast and bake as you normally would. Once the chicken is cooked fully, add a sprinkle of parmesan on top and broil for a couple of minutes until slightly browned.

The Farm House Natural Cheeses

5634 McCallum Rd., Agassiz, VOM 1A3; 604-796-8741
farmhousecheeses.com

The Farm House Natural Cheeses, home of Debra and George Amrein-Boyes, is located in Agassiz in the far northeastern reaches of the Fraser Valley at what feels like the base of the mountains, about 15 minutes before you arrive at the hotbed of tourist activity, Harrison Hot Springs. This part of the Fraser Valley is a prolific growing region for many different types of produce. The super-lush farmlands and country roads in this area are sprinkled with signs for berries, nuts, eggs, and flowers—and antiques. Whenever I arrive at the Farm House Natural Cheeses shop, the first word that pops into my mind

is "quaint." It is, absolutely, but it is also obviously a bustling business. The shop is almost always hopping with locals and tourists alike, all stocking up on fresh cheese, yogurt, and—if you get there at just the right time—the most delicious fresh butter. The butter sells out incredibly quickly, so you don't want to make this your last stop of the day.

Through a window in the shop, you can see the cheesemakers doing what they do best. For head cheesemaker Debra, making cheese started out as a way to help keep the family farm viable. It grew into her passion and ultimately a lifestyle. In fact, she's been internationally recognized for her work. As for every single farmer I have met and spoken to while working on this book, just selling one product, in this case milk, wasn't enough to sustain the farm. They had to add value to the products they were producing by turning them into something else, something that would keep people coming back, something customers couldn't get elsewhere.

Debra will tell you that the key ingredient in any good cheese is great milk, and that starts with very happy goats and cows. Clearly the goats and cows at the Farm House are ecstatic! All of the cheese produced by the Farm House is made from milk

from the animals on their farm, giving them total control from udder to plate. Debra makes her cheese in a classic French style: runny brie, creamy rich camembert, and what I think is the perfect clothbound cheddar—not classically French, but definitely still a classic. The cheeses speak softly but have fantastic personalities; they aren't strong, brash, or overpowering, and I think that really speaks to the personality of the cheesemaker. Obviously made from fine milk from contented animals, the cheese is very sophisticated. Debra is also a best-selling cookbook author. She is truly a wealth of knowledge when it comes to making and cooking with cheese. If Debra is there when you visit, say hello. She has a great story to tell, and if you see George, her very soft-spoken husband, tending to the animals and working on the property as you wander around to meet the goats, the cows, and the farm cats, try to pry a story or two out of him too. He's quite funny and very charming in an old-world kind of way. When Debra isn't on the farm, you can find her, usually with her daughter, selling their products from their Cheese Truck at any number of local farmers markets.

Farm House Artichoke and Spinach Fondue

Fondue is one of my favorite ways to entertain. It is so social and really allows you to have a great visit while you work your way through the pot of cheesy deliciousness. The wine seems to disappear quickly and the conversation flows freely. The preparation and planning for a fondue require a bit of extra effort, but it's worth it. This cheese fondue is my go-to fondue for a great first course, but it can easily be turned into a main by doubling the recipe and adding more dippers. The fun part is deciding what you're going to dip, but the variations are virtually endless. This recipe really showcases the fantastic cheese Debra Amrein-Boyes produces at Farm House Natural Cheeses.

Serves 2 as an appetizer

½ cup grated Farm House Heidi cheese

½ cup grated Farm House gouda

¼ cup grated Farm House fermière

1 tsp all-purpose flour

⅓ cup dry white wine

1 clove garlic, minced

¾ cup chopped spinach

⅓ cup drained and chopped marinated artichoke hearts

¼ cup whipping cream

1. In a medium-size bowl, combine all of the grated cheeses and sprinkle with the flour. Toss to evenly coat, then set aside.

2. Place the wine and garlic in a small saucepan over medium-high heat and bring to a boil. Add the spinach and artichokes. Stir just until the spinach wilts.

3. Turn down the heat to medium-low and stir in the cheeses. Stir constantly until the cheese is stringy and melted completely, and then stir in the cream. Transfer to a fondue pot with a low flame, or keep in the saucepan on low heat until ready to serve.

4. Serve with your choice of dippers:
· Chunks of good crusty bread
· Sliced cooked sausage
· Steamed baby potatoes
· Blanched cauliflower or broccoli florets
· Roasted mushrooms
· Pieces of cooked chicken, beef, or shrimp
· Steamed Brussels sprouts

Chef Bonnie Friesen

Can be found at: Field House Brewing (see page 138).

Chef Bonnie Friesen is the chef-owner of a gourmet catering company, Faspa and Company (faspaandco.com), founded on the idea that cooking locally and in season connects us to a rich communal heritage. The term "Faspa" is a Low German word for a simple Sunday meal of homemade breads, cheeses, and preserves. Essentially it's a celebration of food and a gathering of friends. For Chef Bonnie, living in the Fraser Valley—surrounded by such stunning landscape and witnessing firsthand how our world-class rivers and the runoff from our mountain forests work together to produce nutrient-rich terrain for quality food—is a privilege. She says her greatest joy as a chef is not only to be able to work with quality ingredients but also to live in the abundant environment from which it came and work firsthand with the farmers, artisans, and business owners who have a hand in cultivating it all.

Bonnie can be found in the kitchen at Field House Brewing in Abbotsford. From there, she caters events and provides the great food they serve with their beer at the brewery. Bonnie's unwavering passion for all things local is evident in every dish she prepares. Her food is fine—really fine, not delicate or precious, but pretty and somehow precise; you can tell a woman made it. It's also delicious. The flavors are refined and the presentation is whimsical. I'm always surprised by something when I eat Bonnie's food. She has a great imagination for presentation and a flair for turning a basic ingredient into something really special. In short, her food is outstanding. Go see her at Field House. It's a winning combination.

Yarrow Meadows Duck Confit

Duck confit is a dish and a method. To "confit" is an ancient preservation method of salt-curing meat and cooking it in its own fat. The method is now used for all kinds of things, but duck is still the most common. This recipe from Chef Bonnie is a great way to impress people at a dinner party, so double or triple the recipe and call your friends!

Serves 2

4–6 whole cloves

½ tsp whole black peppercorns

3 tsp kosher salt

2 duck legs (about 1 lb in total)

1 bay leaf, halved

1 stick cinnamon, halved

2 sprigs thyme

2 cloves garlic, smashed

3 cups duck fat

1. To cure the duck legs, crush the cloves and peppercorns with the back of a chef's knife or in a mortar and pestle, and stir to combine. Massage 1 ½ tsp of the salt into the skin and flesh of each duck leg. Place the legs in a nonreactive dish skin side down. Divide the clove and pepper mixture between the two legs and rub it onto the meat. On each leg, place half a bay leaf, half a cinnamon stick, 1 thyme sprig, and 1 garlic clove. Cover the dish with plastic wrap and allow to cure in the refrigerator for at least 24 hours, or up to 48 hours.

2. Once the legs have cured, rinse off the aromatics and excess salt under cold water and pat dry with paper towel.

3. Preheat the oven to 200°F.

4. In an ovenproof casserole dish, place the dried legs in a single layer, skin side up. In a saucepan over medium heat, warm the duck fat until it is liquefied, then pour it over the legs to submerge them completely. Cover the dish with a tight-fitting lid or aluminum foil and cook the legs for 6 to 8 hours.

5. Check on the legs periodically to make sure the fat isn't boiling; turn down the heat if necessary. When the duck is finished, the skin will have completely shrunk off the drumstick bone, and the meat will be very tender and pull away easily from the bone. The meat will be fully cooked inside.

6. Once the legs and fat have cooled slightly, gently remove the legs from the fat, place them in a dish with a tight-fitting lid, and transfer to the refrigerator. Strain the fat into a separate dish and let cool, either covered or uncovered, in the refrigerator as well. Once the fat solidifies, the duck stock will have separated from the fat and settled at the bottom. Depending on the depth of your dish, this could take several hours, so this isn't a last-minute kind of thing to make. Carefully separate the fat, and save the gelatinous stock for soups or sauces, or freeze for future use.

7. In a saucepan over low heat, gently rewarm the fat and pour it back over the cooled duck legs so that they're completely submerged, and cover with a tight-fitting lid or aluminum foil. You can store the confit this way, in the refrigerator, tightly covered, for up to 6 months. The confit will develop a richer flavor over time.

8. To use the confit, gently lift the legs out of the fat. Save the fat for later use (freeze if desired). Heat a frying pan over medium-high heat, then add the legs skin side down to crisp and turn golden brown. Lower the heat and flip the legs over to gently warm the meat, about 5 minutes.

Duck Confit and Beet Salad

This is Chef Bonnie Friesen's go-to salad recipe. I've divided all the components into their own mini-recipes after the main recipe so you can mix and match and use them in other ways.

Serves 2

Salad

2 legs duck confit (see page 196)

1 cup quartered spiced beets

2–3 Tbsp apple cider thyme vinaigrette

4 Tbsp chive crème fraîche

4 Tbsp brown butter rye crumble

3 cups greens, such as peppery arugula

4 Tbsp chèvre

Salt and pepper

1. Preheat the oven to 400°F.

2. In a frying pan over medium-high heat, sear the duck legs until the skin is golden and crispy. Turn down the heat and continue to heat until the meat is warmed through.

3. Toss the beets with 1 Tbsp of the vinaigrette and roast in the oven until caramelized.

4. Spread 2 Tbsp chive crème fraîche on each plate, and sprinkle each with 2 Tbsp rye crumble. Toss the greens with 1 to 2 Tbsp vinaigrette, season with salt and pepper, and divide them evenly between the two plates. Top with the beets. Crumble 2 Tbsp chèvre over each salad, and finish with a crisp seared duck confit leg on each one.

Spiced Beets
Makes enough for 2 salads

3 medium-size golden or purple beets

3 Tbsp apple cider vinegar

1 Tbsp sugar

2 tsp salt

1 whole pod green cardamom

1 whole clove

⅛ tsp whole black peppercorns

⅛ tsp fennel seeds

1. Trim the ends off the beets, but do not peel them. Place all the ingredients in a large pot, cover completely with water, and bring to a boil, uncovered, over high heat. Turn down the heat to medium and simmer until the beets pierce easily with a knife, about 20 minutes.

2. Strain and allow to cool. The skin will peel away easily. Quarter the beets and set aside until needed.

3. Peeled cooked beets can be stored in an airtight container in the refrigerator for up to 4 days.

Apple Cider Thyme Vinaigrette
Makes ½ cup

2 Tbsp apple cider vinegar

½ tsp Dijon mustard

½ tsp minced shallots

¼ tsp roughly chopped thyme leaves

Salt and pepper

6 Tbsp extra virgin olive oil

1. Whisk together the vinegar, mustard, shallots, and thyme. Add a pinch of salt and pepper. While whisking, stream in the olive oil. Season to taste.

2. Leftover vinaigrette can be stored in an airtight container in the refrigerator for up to 10 days and used on a variety of salads.

Chive Crème Fraîche
Makes 1 cup

1 cup whipping cream

1 Tbsp full-fat buttermilk

2 Tbsp minced shallots

½ tsp minced fresh chives

Salt and pepper

1. Combine the cream and buttermilk in a nonreactive dish, cover with cheesecloth, and let sit at room temperature for 24 hours.

2. Once the crème fraîche has thickened, place it in the refrigerator for 2 hours to set. Store it in the refrigerator for up to 2 weeks.

3. To make chive crème fraîche, stir in the shallots and chives. Season to taste with salt and pepper. Leftover chive crème fraîche can be stored in an airtight container in the refrigerator for up to 1 week (and is delicious on baked potatoes).

Brown Butter Rye Crumble
Makes 2 cups

2 cups (1-inch) day-old rye bread cubes

¼ cup unsalted butter

½ tsp salt

1. Line a baking sheet with parchment paper.

2. In a food processor fitted with the steel blade, pulse the rye bread until it has a fine crumb consistency.

3. In a large frying pan over medium heat, melt the butter. Once it begins to bubble, stir constantly until the butter begins to toast and smell nutty. Add the rye crumbs and stir to absorb the butter. Continue to stir until the crumbs are well toasted and a deep golden brown. Season with the salt.

4. Remove from the heat and let cool on the prepared baking sheet.

5. Store rye crumble in an airtight container at room temperature for up to 2 weeks. Leftover crumble is great sprinkled on pasta, or over salad instead of croutons.

Chef Rossana Ascencio

Can be found at: Farmers markets and specialty stores all over BC and teaching classes at Well Seasoned in Langley.
omgfoods.ca

Chef Rossana Ascencio is the founder and owner of Encanto Culinary Services and the co-creator of OMG Foods, where they make traditional Mexican cajeta (ka-heh-tah) with Happy Days Dairy goat milk (see page 177). OMG cajeta is a reduction of goat milk, cooked for hours and without the addition of butter or whipping cream. It's like a traditional caramel or dulce de leche. Rossana takes the time to caramelize the milk, not the sugar, and the result is a heavenly, super-addictive sauce in three different flavors: vanilla—made with Mexican vanilla beans, of course— espresso, and rum. If you have a sweet tooth but you've never had cajeta, it's definitely something you should experience. And the natural sweet-ness that comes from the caramelization of the milk makes it a fantastic sweet treat without any added refined syrups or artificial ingredients. Try it on a dry piece of multigrain toast instead of jam or on hot oatmeal with sliced apples, or, for a treat at happy hour, mix Kahlúa, cajeta, and fresh milk over ice.

While you might think OMG stands for "oh my god" it's good, it actually stands for "original Mexican gourmet"—but really, I think they're interchangeable.

Alongside OMG Foods, Chef Rossana runs a booming catering business, Encanto Culinary Services (culinaryencanto.com). She specializes in Mexican cuisine and makes the best tamales and enchiladas you've ever had and a ceviche that will make you weep. Her food is authentic, and her love for Mexican food and culture is evident in everything she does. When she teaches cooking classes at Well Seasoned, she even brings her dad along. He likes to "supervise" and share his great stories with the guests in the class. (Try her Chiles Rellenos con Mole de Avellana on page 178.)

Cajeta Slide

This is a very grown-up dessert cocktail from Chef Rossana. I like to serve it at Christmastime instead of eggnog.

Serves 1

1 Tbsp cajeta (rum or espresso flavor) + 1 tsp to drizzle inside the glass

2 oz vodka

1 oz Kahlúa

1 oz whipping cream, milk, or almond or soy milk

Ice cubes

For a frozen Cajeta Slide, mix all the ingredients, including the ice, in a blender and serve in a tall glass drizzled with cajeta. Top with whipped cream and drizzle with more cajeta.

1. Use a spoon or a squeeze bottle to drizzle the 1 tsp of the cajeta inside a rocks glass. It will look so pretty when you fill the glass.

2. In a cocktail shaker, combine the vodka, Kahlúa, cream, and 1 Tbsp cajeta with lots of ice and shake vigorously to combine. Pour into the cajeta-drizzled glass and drizzle more cajeta on top if you like. Serve immediately.

Other Places to Visit

Bravo Restaurant and Lounge

46224 Yale Rd., Chilliwack, V2P 2P5; 604-792-7721

The food speaks for itself. Fine dining, creative cocktails, a beautiful wine list, and a menu featuring local products. Make a reservation and book a hotel nearby for a very romantic evening out. (bravorestaurant.ca)

Chaos and Solace Craft Brewing Co.

9360 Mill St., Chilliwack, V2P 4N2; 604-391-1000

There is always something interesting brewing here. Jalapeño Kolsch, Raspberry Bourbon Porter, Vanilla Cocoa Nib Hazelnut Porter, and Sour Saffron Saison are just a few examples of how these guys are innovating with local beer. (chaosandsolace.com)

The Yellow Deli

45859 Yale Rd., Chilliwack, V2P 2N6; 604-702-4442

Open 24 hours a day, 5 days a week, the Yellow Deli makes all of the food you would expect to find in a great neighborhood deli café, and they make it well, from scratch, with locally sourced ingredients. They are open from Sunday at noon until Friday at 3:00 p.m. If you can come up with a description for this place other than "unique," please let me know! (yellowdeli.com/chilliwack)

The Curly Kale Eatery

5669 Vedder Rd., Chilliwack, V2R 3N3; 604-845-5643

Local, organic food made with love. They're closed Sundays and they don't have a website, but you can find them on Facebook @curlykaleeatery or call them. They are absolutely worth a visit when you're in the 'Wack.

Fishing on the Fraser River

604-792-3544

Catch your dinner! Fishing on the Fraser is an adventurer's dream come true. You can "chase the dinosaurs" and try your hand catching and releasing a white sturgeon, or you can charter a boat and get your limit of wild salmon. There is no experience like it. If you have the time and inclination, it's a once-in-a-lifetime experience to be in the water with an experienced guide. (greatriverfishing.com)

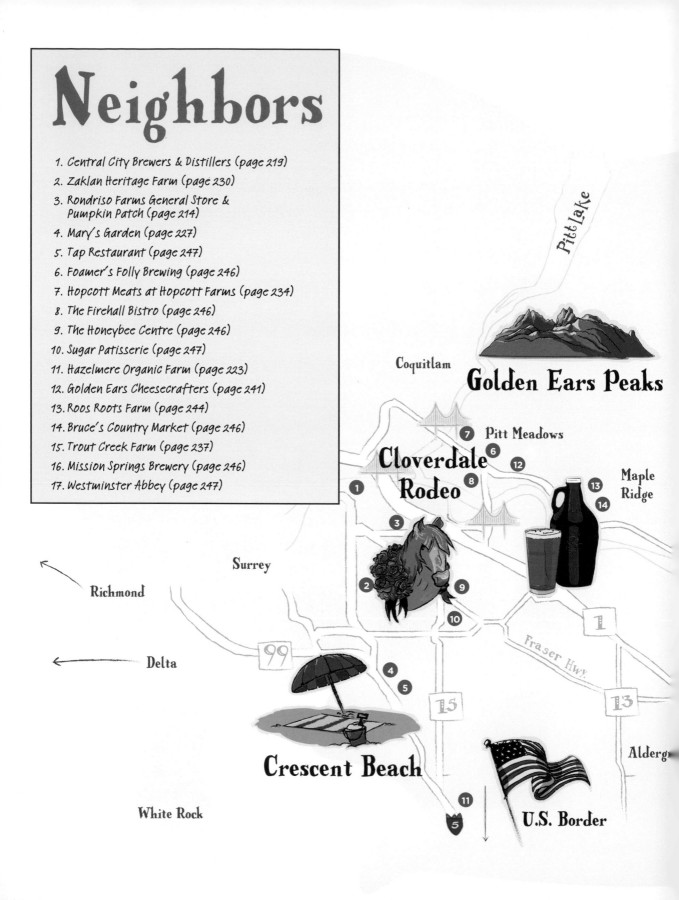

Neighbors

Pitt Lake

Coquitlam

Golden Ears Peaks

Cloverdale Rodeo

Pitt Meadows

Maple Ridge

Surrey

Richmond

Delta

99

Fraser Hwy.

1

15

13

Crescent Beach

White Rock

U.S. Border

Alderg

Alouette Lake

Stave Lake

Harrison Lake

Hope

**Harrison
Hot Springs**

Fraser River

**Westminster
Abbey**

Harrison River

9

1

Chilliwack

15

17

Mission

7

16

11

Fraser River

FRASER VALLEY
+LOWER MAINLAND

Neighbors

Just as you're about to cross the Port Mann Bridge as you drive east from Vancouver to Hope, you have a very important choice to make: to turn north or stay the course. Decisions, decisions, decisions . . .

Surrey

When you choose to head south, Surrey is the first stop as you cross the Port Mann bridge heading east to the Fraser Valley. Surrey is huge, spanning 122 square miles, about one-third of which is agricultural land. It is not a suburb of Vancouver; it is a thriving metropolis finding its own identity. About half a million people call it home, and for good reason—it's a great community. Accessible by SkyTrain and rapid transit, it's full of urban adventures with all of the conveniences and amenities you expect from a big city.

It's also a city of change. As the urban needs of the community grow, so too does the pressure on the suburban lands and farms. The majority of farms left in Surrey are now large and greenhouse-based or producing massive quantities of produce for local and international markets. The small family farms and niche organic farms have been moved farther east. The ones that remain in Surrey are doing well on family land, but the urban encroachment and changing landscape are both very obvious. In addition, it has parks, lakes, and, of course, the Pacific Ocean!

As you explore Surrey, you'll quickly discover that it is made up of six distinct communities: Cloverdale, Fleetwood, Guildford, Newton, North Surrey, and South Surrey. They each offer a different flavor and feel, and all are well worth exploring. For more than 70 years, Cloverdale has been famous for its rodeo. On the May long weekend each year, you can watch one of Canada's greatest outdoor shows and attend the Country Fair. Cowboys from all over North America compete at this fun family

event. The kids can ride on the midway, play games, listen to great country music, eat a foot-long 'dog, and meet the animals in the petting zoo. You can buy tickets in advance and plan your weekend so you don't miss out on anything—especially the mutton busting. It's hilarious! (See cloverdalerodeo.com.)

Fleetwood, Guildford, and Newton are loaded with parks, shopping, and restaurants. It's fun to explore the communities and discover the farms that remain on their outer boundaries, like Rondriso and the Honeybee Centre (honeybeecentre.com) in the eastern reaches of Fleetwood.

In North Surrey, you'll discover the urban heart of the city. In Holland Park, you can participate in the city's Fusion Festival, Children's Festival, or the Surrey Urban Farmers Market (surrey-market.org), and after all of that, you can have a great meal and a cold beer at Central City Brewers and Distillers.

South Surrey is stunning. In the southwestern reaches of the area, you will find Crescent Beach, a small historic beach community. You can swim at Blackie Spit, join a game of beach volleyball, beachcomb, or walk your dog and window-shop through town. You'll want to stop for lunch or dinner at the iconic Seahorse Grill or eat fish and chips while sitting on a log facing the sea. You can watch a sunset at White Rock, walk the pier while eating ice cream cones, or build a sandcastle or beachcomb while the tide is out.

Surrey has a lot to offer and is a terrific place to start your Fraser Valley adventures (especially if you're coming from the US), but don't be too distracted by all of the

Tourist information:
discoversurreybc.com

bright, shiny stuff staring you right in the face as you drive down the highway—the farmgates and artisan food producers are slightly off the beaten path, but more than worth the effort to track down.

Pitt Meadows, Maple Ridge, and Mission

If you choose to head north, follow the signs for Highway 7 (Lougheed Highway). They'll lead you to the Fraser Valley's incredibly friendly neighbors on the north side of the Fraser River, where you'll find a stunning array of farms, farmgates, breweries, artisans, and natural attractions definitely worth a visit. Pitt Meadows, Maple Ridge, and Mission are a combined population of about 85,000. It's a stunning part of the region. Although they are three separate, distinctly different municipalities, they share the beautiful geography of the Golden Ears peaks, the twin summits of the Coast Mountain range you'll see to the north of Maple Ridge. (Many locals often refer to them simply as the Golden Ears—or even the Ears.)

Sometimes when I look across the Fraser River and gaze toward my neighbors, I feel like an old man, propping myself up to look over the fence because I smell the smoke of a BBQ, peering into the neighbor's backyard and wondering what fun things they're up to. The grass isn't actually greener on the north side of the river, but sometimes it feels that way—usually when it's raining south of the river and the sun's out north of it. Between the Fraser River and the Golden Ears lie lush farms, fish hatcheries, lakes, rivers, hiking trails, cheeseries, breweries, and wineries. You can easily spend just as much time exploring the north side of the river as you do the south. You can ride your bike on the dikes; canoe or fly-fish in the Pitt River; play a round of golf; or fish for the ancient sturgeon, freshwater Dolly Varden, or trout. If you're feeling adventurous, you could embark on a search for the elusive Slumach's Gold. Remember me if you find it!

For a day trip, visit Pitt Lake, North America's largest tidal freshwater lake and one of the deepest (read: coldest) lakes in the world. Do check the tides before you launch any watercraft, though. Afterward, pop down to Osprey Village—a real gem tucked away between the Fraser and the highway. The neighbors' backyard really is an amazing place to explore!

When you're on this side of the river, you must plan to spend a day at Golden Ears Provincial Park and Alouette Lake. It is *the* perfect place for a day trip, picnic in hand, to enjoy a refreshing swim on a hot summer day or go for a hike in the shade of the trees. You can rent a canoe or kayak and explore the lake from the water. The water at Alouette Lake is crisp and clear, and you'll find shaded picnic areas just beyond the sandy beach, sprinkled with picnic tables. BBQs are welcome (but check for restrictions in summer if the forest-fire level is high). (And you might spot a film crew while you're there.) Before you head up to the lake, stop to fill a growler at Foamers' Folley (foamersfolly.ca) and pick up sandwiches and picnic fixings at Hopcott Meats

Tourist information

Pitt Meadows: pittmeadows.bc.ca

Maple Ridge: www.mapleridge.ca

Mission: mission.ca

(hotcottmeats.ca) in Pitt Meadows. Golden Ears isn't just incredible in the summer; during the winter months, you can snowshoe and explore the trails, but the park gates close early, so check the website before you head up.

If you don't have any pets with you, you could also stretch your legs on one of the trails in the Malcolm Knapp Research Forest (www.mkrf.forestry.ubc.ca). If you do have your dog with you, there are numerous other parks in the area where you can walk together.

As you continue to drive east on Highway 7 from Pitt Meadows to Mission, you'll follow the Fraser River and ultimately end up in Hope, where you can circle back west through the Fraser Valley and back to Vancouver. But don't rush off home just yet; you'll want to stop a while in Mission. If you don't fancy a round of golf or a walk on one of the many trails, you can watch the bald eagles fish for salmon or visit the Westminster Abbey and the Benedictine monks. The abbey is in the hills above Mission City, and the view from the monastery is spectacular. The bell tower has a ring of ten bells that sound 15 minutes before each mass. The very popular Sunday mass, held in one of Canada's most beautiful places of worship, is at 10:00 a.m., but be advised that shorts are not allowed in the chapel.

All of that is sure to make you hungry and thirsty, so a stop at the Mission Springs Brewing Company (missionsprings.ca) is definitely in order—a tourist needs to keep their strength up!

A drive through this region, along the Fraser, will make it abundantly clear why they call BC Super Natural!

Tourist information for the region:
hellobc.com and scenic7bc.com
Facebook: @HelloBC
Instagram: @hellobc
Twitter: @HelloBC

Rondriso Farms General Store and Pumpkin Patch

8390 – 172nd St., Surrey, V4N 3G4; 604-574-5585
rondrisofarms.ca

Rondriso Farms is tucked tightly between Surrey's urban sprawl and Highway 17 with barely an inch to move. The Tamis family has been farming in Surrey since 1958, long before anyone even knew what urban sprawl was, when Surrey and the rest of the Fraser Valley were mostly farmland. The Rondriso General Store is just a few steps down the driveway, where you'll find ample parking and from where, even if you can't see them, you can smell the cows. Standing in the parking lot in my rubber boots on a rainy Saturday morning, I kept thinking how lucky the neighborhood is to have such a fantastic working farm, harvesting non-GMO sweet corn, potatoes, squash, beets, onions, etc., basically in its backyard. And then I quickly realized that they probably get more complaints than praise, as some of their new neighbors are probably less tolerant of the smells and sounds of a working farm. If you take a few minutes to look around and pause to think, it's easy to see the challenges a family farm faces as urban sprawl creeps closer and closer.

But back to the food! Unable to resist the veggies still wet from the ground, I filled my bag. The purple onions are the sweetest and most delicious I have ever had. The beet greens needed only a quick steam, a little butter, and some salt to turn them into healthy perfection on my plate. It's easy to see why the fingerling

potatoes and other root veggies are very much in demand with the local chefs—they're perfect! The cows you can hear and smell are Simmental cattle, raised on grass, finished on grain, and sold exclusively through the farm—but only if you preorder. (Psssst: You should do that!)

On October 1, the Rondriso Pumpkin Patch opens. You can take a hayride from the farmgate down to the pumpkin field, where you can pick out your own pumpkins—and for the décor-conscious, Pinterest-posting pumpkin pickers, there are even white ones! After choosing the perfect pumpkin, you can have a little visit with the cows and chickens before shopping the market for other tasty supplies. Rondriso Farms is a great place to visit all year, but is really special in the fall. Plan to spend several hours if you're visiting the pumpkin patch. You can't rush perfection!

Rondriso Purple Onion Soup

I love my onion soup recipe, and I've been making it for years. Onion soup makes a perfect fall supper, especially ideal after you've spent the day pumpkin picking. The purple onions from Rondriso are super-sweet and add so much flavor to the dish, but really, any type of onion can make a great soup; you might just need to add a wee bit more sugar if you are using regular yellow onions or onions that are not quite as freshly picked.

Serves 8

4 Tbsp olive oil + more for brushing

3 lb purple onions, stems removed, peeled, and thinly sliced

2 Tbsp unsalted butter

1 Tbsp brown sugar

1 tsp salt + more to taste

2 cloves garlic, minced

½ cup dry white wine

8 cups beef or rich vegetable stock

3 sprigs thyme

2 bay leaves

½ tsp freshly ground black pepper

8 (1-inch-thick) slices French-style bread

Pepper

2 Tbsp brandy

1½ cups grated swiss or gruyère

¼ cup grated parmesan

1. In a large heavy-bottomed saucepan over medium heat, heat 3 Tbsp of the olive oil. Add the onions and toss to coat with the olive oil. Cook the onions, stirring often, until they soften and are barely starting to brown, about 20 minutes.

2. Increase the heat to medium-high. Add the remaining olive oil and the butter and cook, stirring often, until the onions start to brown, about 15 more minutes. Then sprinkle with the sugar and 1 tsp salt and continue to cook, stirring often, until the onions are nicely caramelized and golden brown, about 15 more minutes.

3. Add the garlic and then the wine to deglaze the pot, scraping all of the brown bits off the bottom. Add the stock, thyme, and bay leaves. Bring to a simmer, cover, and turn down the heat to low so it simmers slowly for 45 minutes.

4. When the soup is almost done simmering, preheat the oven to 450°F with a rack in the upper third of the oven.

5. With a silicone brush, brush both sides of the French bread slices lightly with olive oil. Put them on a sheet pan and toast in the oven until lightly browned, 3 to 4 minutes per side. Remove the toasts from the oven and set aside.

6. When the soup is done simmering, remove the lid, taste the broth, and season to taste with more salt and the pepper. Remove and discard the bay leaves and thyme sprigs, and stir in the brandy. Ladle the soup into ovenproof bowls and place a slice of toasted bread into the center of each soup bowl so it floats. Sprinkle the toasts generously with the grated swiss and parmesan cheeses. Place the filled soup bowls on a sheet pan and return them to the oven to bake until the cheese is bubbly and starting to brown. Remove the sheet pan from the oven and allow the soup to rest for a few minutes before serving.

Onions 101: Yellow onions are the most popular for cooking because they are very accessible and add an excellent flavor to most cooked dishes. Typically, when a recipe calls for onions, a yellow onion will always work. White onions have a milder flavor than other onions and are often used in raw applications where you don't want the onion to overpower everything else, like in a fresh salsa. Red and purple onions are generally the mildest and sweetest, so they work great in salads and on sandwiches. The fresher any onion is, the sweeter it is—strong onion flavors and sometimes bitterness start to develop as the onion ages. Onions are best stored in a dry, dark, cool place, not the refrigerator.

Central City Brewers and Distillers

11411 Bridgeview Dr., Surrey, V3R 2N1; 604-588-2337
centralcitybrewing.com

I've been a fan of the Red Racer beer brewed at Central City since their humble beginnings in 2003, and it has been so great to watch them grow into leaders in the local craft beer industry. Based in Surrey, Central City started brewing beer in the heart of Whalley with a single brewpub, where they made and served their beer alongside some really great food. The original Surrey Centre location still exists just off King George Highway, but it's no longer their production facility. That has moved to a brand-new, state-of-the-art brewery and distillery on Bridgeview Drive, also in Surrey.

Ten years after they started making great craft beer, Central City decided that by abiding by the same philosophy for quality, they could create some phenomenal small-batch spirits, and with that, the Central City distillery was born. It now produces a London Dry–style Queensborough gin. Their Seraph vodka is distilled from 100 percent BC malted barley.

You know the saying "a rolling stone gathers no moss"? Well, that has apparently never been truer than when describing the creative juices that flow at Central City. Always evolving and innovating, they have added a wicked good summer libation to their portfolio, a craft cider radler, the first one ever produced in Canada. As you probably know, a radler is traditionally a blend of beer and grapefruit juice, but these guys have taken their Hopping Mad Dry Hopped Apple Cider and added grapefruit juice to create the super-tasty Hopping Mad Cider Radler, the quintessential breakfast beverage. You may never have another mimosa! It's a bit like beer, a little like cider, a little fruit juicy, gluten-free, super-refreshing, and dangerously easy to drink.

The brewery is really worth a visit. You can join one of the Grain to Glass tours offered on weekends, but be sure to pop on the website to confirm the dates and times and to book your space, as they tend to fill up in advance. While Central City is not considered one of the "little guys" anymore, they're still taking chances and innovating, constantly creating new products and seasonal brews. There's definitely something for everyone at Central City. You can find many of their products at local liquor or cold beer and wine stores, but if you want to taste it all, the best place to do that is at one of their brewpubs—the original in Surrey and the newest one in downtown Vancouver both offer a classic pub-style menu meant to highlight the beer, cider, and spirits they have on tap. Remember to take your growler in with you so you can fill it up to enjoy later when you aren't so full!

You can also find them at

Central City Surrey, 13450 – 102nd Ave., Surrey, V3T 2W1

Central City Vancouver, 871 Beatty St., Vancouver, V6B 2M6

Baked Beans with Red Racer Copper Ale

I know most people think of baked beans as a summer thing, but I could eat them all year. If you use dried beans, which I do in this recipe, it takes a bit more time, so feel free to replace the dried beans with two (19 oz) cans of cannellini beans and reduce the cooking time to an hour. I have always made my recipe in an old pottery bean crock I inherited from my grandmother, but any heavy saucepan with a tight-fitting lid—or even a crockpot—will work well. The malt flavors and slight hoppy bitterness of the beer work great with the sweetness of the molasses and brown sugar.

Serves 6 as a side

1 lb dried small white beans, such as navy beans

1 small yellow onion, peeled and halved

1 carrot, peeled and halved

2 cloves garlic, peeled and halved

1 tsp salt

1 bay leaf

½ lb thick-cut bacon, diced

1 large yellow onion, diced

½ cup molasses

2 Tbsp brown sugar

1 Tbsp tomato paste

2 tsp Dijon mustard

1 can (355 mL) Central City Red Racer Copper Ale

Pepper

Hot sauce (optional)

1. In a medium bowl, cover the beans with cold water and let them soak overnight, at least 12 hours or up to 1 day. Drain and rinse.

2. In a medium-size ovenproof saucepan with a tight-fitting lid, over high heat, combine the onions, carrots, garlic, and salt with the presoaked beans and cover them with just enough cool water to submerge them. Bring that to a boil, uncovered, and add the bay leaf. Turn down the heat to medium and simmer the beans until they're tender, about 45 minutes. Drain the beans and discard the carrots, onions, and bay leaf.

3. Preheat the oven to 325°F.

4. Return the saucepan to the stove over medium-high heat and cook the diced bacon until semi-crispy. Drain off most of the excess fat and turn the heat to medium. Add the diced onions, stir to combine, and sauté until very soft and translucent. Add the drained beans, molasses, brown sugar, tomato paste, and mustard along with the can of beer and 2 cups fresh, cool water. Stir to combine, then increase the temperature to high to bring to a boil. Remove from the stove, put the lid on the saucepan, and transfer to the oven.

5. Bake the beans in the covered saucepan until they're soft and tender, about 4 hours. Stir the beans occasionally, adding about ½ cup boiling water at a time if necessary so they don't dry out. Once the beans are tender and the sauce is thick and dark brown, remove from the oven, and season to taste (but note that the bacon might provide enough salt). Add a few drops of hot sauce if you like.

6. Serve the beans warm or refrigerate them for up to a week, adding some water when you reheat if the sauce gets too thick. Keep warm until ready to serve.

Hazelmere Organic Farm

1859 – 184th St., Surrey, V4P 1M6; 604-538-3018
www3.telus.net/hazelmereorganics

Founded by Gary and Naty King in 1984, Hazelmere Organic Farm is one of the best-known, most successful organic farmgates in the Fraser Valley. Farmer Gary, as he was fondly referred to, passed away in 2009, but Naty continues to farm and champion organic, sustainable farming practices and producers from their sprawling 6-acre farm.

Farmer Gary was the first celebrity farmer I ever met. When I first met him, he was supplying produce to the finest restaurants and chefs in Vancouver. Those chefs sang his praises at every opportunity. If farmers could be compared to rock stars, Farmer Gary was South Surrey's own Ringo Starr. In conjunction with John Bishop, from Bishop's Restaurant in Vancouver, the Kings created a program at their farm designed to teach young farmers and culinary students about their sustainable practices for food production, hoping to instill in them the same farm-to-table ideals that John Bishop shared in his restaurant. It worked; the next generation of chefs, and the next generation after that, have all had some contact with Naty King—or Farmer Gary, if they were lucky before he passed—and learned about the importance of connecting the land to their food and of a relationship with their farmers. That exact program doesn't exist now, but fortunately, some of the chefs and farmers who followed the paths of Gary King and John Bishop are creating their own means of sharing the knowledge and educating the next generation.

Hazelmere doesn't just carry Hazelmere's own products and produce. It carries more than 300 organic products. Many are local, but there are also lines of spices, seasonings, and chocolate that come from organic farms all over the world. From frozen food to canned goods, meat to soup to nuts, this place has literally everything you can eat. Naty brings fresh produce and products in from a ton of other local farms every week, giving you the very best variety any season has to offer, every day of the year.

Hazelmere Brussels Sprout Caesar Salad

This is a great way to enjoy fresh-from-the-farm Brussels sprouts in a salad. The small ones are tender and have great flavor. Even people who think they hate Brussels sprouts like my salad. (Right, Dad?) The bigger the sprouts get, the more they seem to resemble cabbage and, I think, the better they cook.

Serves 6

Caesar Dressing
2 egg yolks

Juice of 2 lemons

3 cloves garlic, minced

1 tsp Worcestershire sauce

8 anchovy fillets or 1 Tbsp anchovy paste

1 cup finely grated parmesan + 2 Tbsp for garnish

1 tsp red wine vinegar

¼ tsp cayenne pepper

½ cup extra virgin olive oil

Salt and pepper

Salad
2 lb Brussels sprouts

1 cup chopped flat-leaf parsley

3 cups croutons

½ cup chopped, crisp-cooked bacon

1. For the dressing, in a food processor or blender, blend the egg yolks, lemon juice, garlic, Worcestershire, anchovies, 1 cup parmesan, vinegar, and cayenne until smooth. With the machine running, slowly add the olive oil in a thin, steady stream. The dressing will start to thicken and emulsify. When it's fully blended, stop the machine and taste. Adjust the seasoning with salt and pepper to taste and blend again just to combine. The dressing should be slightly acidic but really savory.

2. For the salad, trim the stems off the Brussels sprouts and remove any wilted or discolored leaves. Cut each sprout in half, then slice each half into strips as you would do cabbage for coleslaw.

3. In a large bowl, mix together the sliced sprouts, parsley, and croutons. Toss with the Caesar dressing. Garnish with the chopped bacon and remaining parmesan, and serve right away.

The Caesar dressing will keep well in an airtight container in the refrigerator for up to 3 days. To prevent the greens from going soggy, dress your salad just before you're ready to serve it.

Mary's Garden

15649 – 40th Ave., Surrey, V3S 0L2; 604-576-9297
marysgarden.ca

Since 1966, the Nootebos family has been growing fresh food for their community, and they've been doing it right. On their South Surrey farm they grow an ever-changing variety of produce, but you can always find their staples: new potatoes, onions, kale, at least five different kinds of lettuce, beets, peppers, chard, spinach, beans, squash, herbs, and radishes. On a warm day, late in the afternoon, you can smell the basil as soon as you get out of your car. At Mary's, you can count on filling your shopping bags to the brim with high-quality produce at an incredibly fair price (fair to both the producer and the consumer—does it get any better?). Fruit and veggies from other farms in the Fraser Valley as well as from the Okanagan and the BC Interior fill their shelves through the summer, all clearly identified with their place of origin so you know exactly what you're buying and where it came from. This is *the* place in Surrey to stock up on your canning peaches and tomatoes, and pickling cukes and beets. Fresh veggies are harvested and sold all day, 6 days a week from late spring through fall, and if you take a minute to stand back and people-watch for a few minutes, you'll likely spot a local chef or two deciding on the finishing touches for their menus that night.

There's nothing fancy about Mary's—it's a working farm with a busy market— but the food is real, fresh, and local, and I'll take that over fancy-schmancy any day. When you visit, if they have their homegrown, fresh radishes, do yourself a favor and buy a few bunches. Yes, a few, more than one. It was after a visit to Mary's Garden about 20 years ago that I first discovered the simple pleasure of buttered radishes. I had stumbled over them online—I think the Barefoot Contessa was preparing them for her husband—and it made me insanely curious. Sliced raw radishes slathered with butter—that's weird. It's actually incredibly weird, but also incredibly delicious. A thick slice of fresh baguette very generously buttered with fresh local (or homemade) butter, piled with thinly sliced fresh radishes and a sprinkling of sea salt will change the way you think about radishes. You can forgo the bread and just dip the raw radishes right into the butter, but don't forget the salt. They need it. I used to think radishes were almost completely useless—I mean, how many can you eat in a salad?—but a newfound appreciation was born after that visit to Mary's. There's plenty for you to discover at Mary's Garden, and you'll be glad you went a little out of your way to do so.

Butter-Braised Radishes

Radishes, like most other root vegetables, benefit from a little braising, some fat, and some salt. My recipe is simple, but the cooking really highlights the intense pepperiness of the radishes and the richness of the butter braise sweetens the whole dish up a little—a totally different experience than eating them raw with butter as mentioned on the previous page.

Serves 4 as a side

1 cup water

6 Tbsp unsalted butter

1 lb radishes, topped (about 2 bunches)

Salt

6–8 sprigs dill, finely chopped

1. In a large frying pan over high heat, bring the water and butter to a boil. Add the radishes and cover with a tight-fitting lid. Turn down the heat to low and allow the radishes to simmer until they're fork-tender, about 15 minutes.

2. Remove the lid from the pan and increase the temperature to medium-high. Cook, uncovered, for about another 5 minutes, until most of the liquid has evaporated and disappeared. The radishes will be glistening from the butter and the pan just slightly moist.

3. Turn off the heat, transfer the radishes with their juices to a serving bowl, season with salt, and garnish with fresh dill.

Radish leaves are totally edible, so don't just fire them into the compost.
Give them a cool water bath and a spin dry and add a few to
your favorite salad mix. The leaves are just as peppery as the radish bulb,
so you can add them to boost the flavor when you're making
a pesto or to liven up your sautéed spinach.

Zaklan Heritage Farm

13278 – 84th Ave., Surrey, V3W 3G9; 604-355-1061
zaklanheritagefarm.com

Doug Zaklan and Gemma McNeill are young farmers who met at the Centre for Sustainable Food Systems at the UBC Farm School, and in 2013 they began farming together on the 8 acres of land that Doug's grandparents, Dragan and Marta Zaklan, started farming in the 1920s. With support from the whole Zaklan family, Doug and Gemma have since transformed the property into a diverse vegetable and livestock operation. On the Zaklan Heritage Farm, they grow more than 40 different types of vegetables and have become especially well known for their salad greens, tomatoes, and root veg. Oh, and eggs, fresh eggs from about 100 free-range chickens.

The farm is truly a magical spot; their customers always tell them it is like an oasis in the middle of the city. It's located in the heart of Surrey and surrounded by houses; most people have no idea it even exists. People are always amazed there's so much food growing right in their neighborhood!

About 20 percent of the produce from the farm is sold through their Community Supported Agriculture (CSA) program—essentially a partnership between farmers and members that gives farmers a guaranteed income and consumers a guaranteed supply. The rest of the farm's produce is sold at their weekly farmgate market, at farmers markets, and through a wholesaler that supplies several local restaurants. Doug and Gemma have a growing customer base, one that is keen to understand where their food comes from and wants to put as much local food on their tables as possible. To visit the farm or learn where to find their products, check their website. It's loaded with information about their growing philosophy, their CSA boxes, and the list of markets where you can find them if you miss them at the farm.

Tomato Sauce

The Zaklan family has been growing tomatoes for over 80 years, so they kind of know what they are doing when it comes to making sauce! Stock up on tomatoes at the height of tomato season in August and early September and make batches of this sauce to keep in the freezer and enjoy all winter long. The carrots add sweetness and mellow out some of the tomato's acidity. This is great with pasta.

Makes about 16 cups

6 Tbsp extra virgin olive oil

2 red onions, chopped

4 carrots, chopped

3 cloves garlic, minced

8 lb vine-ripened tomatoes, skin left on, coarsely chopped (about 10 large tomatoes)

2 Tbsp tomato paste

3 tsp sugar

1 tsp salt

1 Tbsp pepper

1 tsp dried red chili flakes

½ cup packed chopped basil leaves

1. Heat the olive oil in a large heavy-bottomed saucepan over medium-low heat. Add the onions and carrots and sauté for about 10 minutes, until very tender. Add the garlic and cook for 1 minute. Add the tomatoes, tomato paste, sugar, salt, pepper, chili flakes, and chopped basil. Turn down the heat to low and let simmer, uncovered, for 30 minutes, until the vegetables are very tender.

2. At this point, you can put the mixture through a food mill. The mill will extract the tomato skins and seeds and make the sauce smooth. If you don't have a food mill and are not fussy about the seeds and skins, a food processor will work to purée the sauce.

3. Allow the sauce to cool completely, then transfer to airtight containers and freeze for up to 1 year.

Tomato Soup

The Zaklan family use their own tomato sauce in their tomato soup. It's an ideal warm-up after a walk in the rain! (Yes, sometimes it rains in the beautiful Fraser Valley . . .)

Makes about 7 cups

4 cups homemade tomato sauce (page 231)

2 cups chicken stock

1 cup whipping cream

1 small bunch basil leaves, thinly sliced

1. In a saucepan over medium heat, place the tomato sauce, stock, and cream. Bring to a gentle boil, then turn down the heat to low to warm it through. Stir in the basil and serve.

Creamy Garlic Scape Dip

Scapes are the flowering shoots of garlic and are one of those specialty items that you can get only for a short window in the spring. This recipe is a springtime staple for the folks at Zaklan Heritage Farm. If you omit the yogurt and mayo, you can use it in place of pesto on pasta, and, of course, it makes a great dip for crackers and veggies.

Makes about 1 cup

10 garlic scapes

¼ cup grated parmesan or asiago, or a mix

¼ cup raw almonds

2 Tbsp roasted sunflower seeds

2 Tbsp olive oil

Salt and pepper

½ cup Greek yogurt

About 3 Tbsp sour cream and/or mayonnaise

1. Wash the garlic scapes and cut off the ends so you're left with just the tender fragrant spirally parts. Chop them into small pieces. Add everything except the Greek yogurt and sour cream/mayonnaise to the food processor. Pulse until you have a pesto-like consistency.

2. Put the blended ingredients into a small bowl and add the Greek yogurt. Stir to combine. Take half of the pesto-yogurt mixture and put it back in the food processor. Purée until almost smooth. Add back to the small bowl.

3. Finally, mix in the sour cream and/or mayonnaise. (This is totally up to you—you can add as much or as little sour cream/mayonnaise as you want to get your dip to just the right level of creaminess or how garlicky you want it to be.) This dip keeps well in an airtight container in the refrigerator for about 3 days, and it is seriously delicious!

Hopcott Meats at Hopcott Farms

18385 Old Dewdney Trunk Rd., Pitt Meadows, V3Y 2R9; 604-465-7799
hopcottmeats.ca

Hopcott might be *the* best reason to visit Pitt Meadows. Well, there are a ton of other great things to see and do in this beautiful riverside community, but I am totally partial to the super-sexy meat case, the friendly service, the knowledgeable staff, and the very handsome butchers!

Hopcott Meats is a third-generation family-run butcher shop located on the Hopcott family farm (Hopcott Farms), close to the Pitt River Bridge. Over the years, the 125-acre Hopcott farm has seen many transformations: from cattle to corn, to cranberries, and back again. With the cost of land in the region, it is very apparent that cattle ranching would not be realistic, so the Hopcotts have forged long-lasting partnerships with ranchers in the northern interior of BC where the cattle are born and spend the first 9 months of their lives grazing the land. Unlike most beef cattle, the Hopcott cows are never treated with growth hormones or steroids or given any GMO food. At about 9 months of age, the cattle are transported to Pitt Meadows, where they are provided with a pretty pampered lifestyle on the Hopcott farm. They enjoy a diet of grass and non-GMO grain and corn until they're sufficiently fat and ready to be processed. The cattle are then transferred just a few miles down the road to a government-inspected facility to be slaughtered and immediately returned to Hopcott to be processed. The fresh beef is then dry-aged for a minimum of 28 days, ensuring customers can purchase the very best fresh local beef available.

In 2015, the Hopcott family raised the bar completely by building a stunning new farm market store where they sell all of their fantastic beef and tons of other food and groceries from local growers and producers. But seriously, the meat case,

which you can see when you walk in the front door of the market, will take the breath away from any self-respecting carnivore! The entire case is local and completely drool-worthy.

If a trip to Pitt Meadows is in your future, check the website for on-farm activities like a corn maze, the pig races, the petting zoo, the cranberry bog, or the long-table dinners, or just take a stroll through the dahlia garden. If a trip isn't in your schedule, plan one now—bring a cooler and some ice packs. You couldn't possibly leave empty-handed. Hopcott is doing everything right and is run by some of the nicest people you could ever meet.

Super-Creamy Mac and Cheese with Beef Bacon Crumble

Beef bacon—yes, it's a thing. A super-delicious thing that they make at Hopcott and sell sliced in their meat case every day. Beef bacon is made from the same cut of beef used to make pastrami, but it's treated, cured, and smoked the same way pork bacon is made. It kind of reminds me of a cross between bacon and beef jerky. It's delicious, but because it's much leaner than pork bacon, it cooks very quickly, and you don't want to overcook it. I think the beef bacon adds just the right amount of meaty, savory saltiness to my recipe, but feel free to add more—when it comes to adding bacon of any kind, you should never feel shy!

Serves 4 as a main, 6 as a side

3 Tbsp unsalted butter

2½ cups uncooked elbow macaroni

1 cup grated aged cheddar

½ tsp salt

¼ tsp pepper

4 cups whole milk

½ cup whipping cream

8 slices Hopcott beef bacon, cooked and chopped

¼ cup grated parmesan

1. Preheat the oven to 375°F. Melt the butter in a deep 9- × 13-inch baking dish in the oven as it heats up.

2. Stir the uncooked macaroni into the melted butter until well coated. Sprinkle the cheese, salt, and pepper over the macaroni. Pour the milk and cream over the macaroni and cheese. Do not stir.

3. Cover the baking dish with aluminum foil and bake for 50 minutes. Remove the foil from the pan, sprinkle over the bacon chunks and parmesan, and return to the oven, covered with foil, for another 15 minutes to brown.

4. Remove from the oven and allow it to rest for 5 minutes before serving. (Seriously, resist the urge to stir the macaroni or peek under the foil!)

Trout Creek Farm

31474 Townshipline Ave., Mission, V4S 1G4; 604-826-5640
ucatchbc.com

Trout Creek is where great fishing stories begin. For decades, you'll be able to regale your friends and family with the details of the one that got away! Everyone who visits loves this place. Trout Creek Farm has two giant fishin' holes (they call them ponds) full of rainbow trout raised without growth hormones or antibiotics. The ponds are so full, it's virtually impossible to leave without a catch. You literally just turn up and start fishing. They have everything you need to catch the big one—they provide the gear and the bait and will even teach you how to properly cast your line. It's the only place in the region you can fish without a license. You can spend as long as you like at the farm. You pay a small entry fee and, of course, for the fish you catch, but they're delicious, so you better catch a few! They don't do catch and release; you keep what you catch, and you can take your catch home and serve it for supper or, if you like, you can clean it and cook it on site on one of their BBQs in the picnic area! Bring a picnic or your favorite side dishes for the trout and spend the day.

After lunch, you can nap on the lush grass under the willow trees or join the kids for a swing at the park. You'll have plenty of time to kick back, relax, and work on your story about how you caught one so big it almost dragged you in and the heroic measures you took just to save your rod!

There's something so satisfying about cooking your catch almost immediately. You need to have only a few things with you, and since you know you're going to catch some fish here, you might as well come prepared! You should bring a roll of aluminum foil, a couple of onions peeled and sliced into rings, sea salt and cracked black pepper, butter or olive oil, and one lemon sliced into rounds. Lay the deboned trout fillet on top of a few onion rings on a sheet of foil, season and drizzle with oil or a dollop of butter, top with a lemon slice or two, and tightly seal the foil into a pouch. Bake on a preheated grill (about 350°F) for about 20 minutes. You can check the doneness by opening the foil to see if the fish is flaky. Remove from the grill and let it rest for a couple of minutes before eating it right out of the foil pouch.

Quick Pan-Fried Trout

This simple recipe of mine works well with other kinds of fish, but the simplicity of the ingredients really lets the fresh, clean lake-water flavor of the trout shine! This dish would be excellent served with Brown Butter Spaghetti (page 243).

Serves 4

1½ cups fine dry breadcrumbs

1 clove garlic, minced

2 Tbsp chopped flat-leaf parsley

Zest and juice of 1 lemon

½ tsp salt

½ cup Dijon mustard (flavored mustards also work, especially tarragon)

4 side fillets (each 6 oz) fresh trout, skin on, deboned, rinsed, and patted dry

¼ cup olive oil

1. In a wide, shallow, flat dish, like a pie plate, mix together the breadcrumbs, garlic, parsley, lemon zest, and salt.

2. In a small bowl, combine the lemon juice and mustard. With a silicone basting brush, brush the lemon-mustard mixture all over both sides of the fish fillets. Then put the coated fillets into the seasoned breadcrumb mixture and gently press to coat both sides.

3. In a large frying pan over medium-high heat, heat the olive oil. When the oil is hot (the fish should sizzle), gently place the fillets into the pan and cook skin side down for about 6 minutes. Carefully flip the fish over and cook on the other side until the fish is golden brown and crispy and starts to flake when gently poked with the tip of a knife, about another 3 to 4 minutes.

4. Remove the fish from the pan onto paper towels to drain. Transfer the fish to a plate and serve with your favorite sides.

Golden Ears Cheesecrafters

22270 – 128th Ave., Maple Ridge, V4R 2R1; 604-467-0004
cheesecrafters.ca

This is a stop you definitely want to make as you travel through Maple Ridge, and you'll want to ensure you have an ice pack and plenty of room in your cooler to stock up. Golden Ears Cheesecrafters, a family business started by two sisters, Jenna and Emma Davison, is a bustling cheese shop, café, farm, production facility, and country store all rolled into one. All of their cheese is made from cow milk, and you can see the Jersey cows grazing right across the street from the shop. It really can't get a whole lot fresher than that!

The staff are friendly, knowledgeable, and happy to take the time to introduce you to their selection of cheeses—and the best part is that all of the cheeses in the case are available for sampling. The havarti is creamy and smooth, the gouda is nutty and slightly chewy, the brie (the "Queen of Cheese") is soft and rich, the cheese curds are squeaky, and the Jersey blue is appropriately stinky! The shop also stocks all of the accoutrements necessary to build a delicious cheese board, including the board itself. In the freezer section, you'll find house-made macaroni and cheese, take-and-bake brie, and an assortment of sweets and other treats. If you have time for brunch or lunch, the menu is, of course, cheese-centric. They also offer occasional cooking demos, and a high tea on Wednesdays (check the website for reservation information). But whatever you do, don't leave without the butter. Available in 1 lb or

½ lb blocks in salted or unsalted, it might leave you unable to eat "regular" butter again. Fresh cream processed into butter on site means it is just that—fresh! The color seems more yellow than store-bought butter. It's richer somehow, and it has more texture—it's almost cheesy. It's hard to explain, but try it side by side with your regular butter. I think you'll be pleasantly surprised.

Browned Butter

Sometimes called "the most magical fat," browned butter is made from fresh unsalted butter melted over medium heat in a heavy-bottomed frying pan. As it heats, it starts to bubble and foam. The milk solids on the bottom of the pan start to brown, and you'll smell a nutty fragrance. As soon as that starts to happen, whisk it and remove the pan from the heat. It goes from brown butter to black butter very quickly; black butter is less delicious. Allow the butter to cool in the pan and store it in an airtight container in the refrigerator or use it immediately. It's typically used as a drizzle over seafood, like fresh pan-seared scallops, to fry fresh sage leaves, or poured over butternut squash ravioli, but it's particularly excellent when used as the butter ingredient in sweet recipes like cookies or pie crust, or to fry an egg, or generously poured over freshly popped popcorn. I'm sure you'll find a million ways to use it.

Brown Butter Spaghetti with Golden Ears Aged Cheddar and Walnuts

This is essentially my version of buttered noodles for adults. Use it as a side dish or a main. No walnuts? No problem. Try pine nuts, pecans, almonds, or hazelnuts.

Serves 4

½ cup unsalted Golden Ears Cheesecrafters butter

1 lb spaghetti

Reserved pasta water

½ cup grated Golden Ears Cheesecrafters 2-year-old cheddar + more for garnish

Salt and pepper

1 cup chopped roasted walnuts

1 small bunch flat-leaf parsley, roughly chopped

1. Follow the instructions in the sidebar on page 242 to make browned butter with the ½ cup butter.

2. Meanwhile, in a large saucepan of salted boiling water, cook the spaghetti to al dente.

3. Drain the pasta, reserving the water. Put the hot spaghetti in a large ceramic bowl and toss with the browned butter and 2 Tbsp of the hot pasta water. Using tongs, toss the pasta to fully distribute the butter, adding more of the pasta water as needed to cover it all. Sprinkle with the grated cheese, toss to combine, and season to taste.

4. Garnish with the chopped walnuts, fresh parsley, and more cheese. Serve immediately.

Roos Roots Farm

24200 – 116th Ave., Maple Ridge, V4R 1L6; 778-387-7225
Facebook: @Roos-Roots-Farm

Andrew "Roo" Hinton is a chef by trade who decided he wanted to grow food as well as cook it. He went back to school to learn all about plants and farming, and then found a job at an organic farm on Salt Spring Island, where he quickly learned the ropes with the ultimate goal of finding his own place. In 2015, he acquired a 2½-acre noncertified organic farm in Maple Ridge and got to work.

His first growing season, 2016, was super-successful, but in his enthusiasm, he grew more than 80 varieties of fruits and vegetables. That is A LOT, especially for someone who works alone. He learned pretty quickly not to spread himself too thin, but he loved every minute of it.

Andrew sells his food from the farm, in his Community Supported Agriculture (CSA) boxes, and through the Maple Ridge Saturday farmers market. He follows organic growing standards, but has not taken the step to become certified as organic. Organic certification locally seems to be less important to the customers who meet Andrew personally and feel confident that he's growing quality produce in a responsible, sustainable way. They're trusting in the farmer. Organic certification is an expensive process and difficult to maintain, especially as a one-man band.

Andrew works through growing seasons on his farm and part-time as a sous-chef at Chameleon, a farm-to-table restaurant in Maple Ridge (chameleonmapleridge.com). He also supplies the restaurant with his produce all year—maybe it should reclassify itself as farmer-to-table? Chameleon has an open kitchen, so give Andrew a wave if you're there. You can also drop by the farm if you call ahead to make sure he's around.

Wilted Kale

Andrew grows two kinds of kale at Roos: Curly and Red Russian. This is his favorite way to prepare them. They're great on their own in this dish or mixed together. The simplicity—and let's face it, the bacon—makes this an extra-delicious way to eat your greens! I love this recipe with a fried egg on it. And eating kale for breakfast, in my mind, counteracts eating pie at lunch. You're welcome.

Serves 4

¼ lb your favorite bacon, sliced

2 Tbsp unsalted butter

2 leeks, thinly sliced, whites and tender greens only

2 bunches kale (about 1 lb), ribs removed, and sliced

Salt and pepper

1. In a large frying pan over medium-high heat, sauté the bacon, stirring often to start to render the fat and crisp up the bacon. Just as the bacon is starting to crisp, add the butter and the leeks. Sauté the leeks for 2 minutes, then add the kale. The kale may not all fit, depending on the size of your pan, but as it wilts, add more to the pan and stir to mix with the leeks and the bacon.

2. When all of the kale is wilted and coated with the bacon fat and butter, taste and season with salt and pepper as necessary. Depending on the bacon you used, it may already be salty enough. Transfer the wilted greens to a serving dish and serve immediately.

Other Places to Visit

Bruce's Country Market

23963 Lougheed Hwy., Maple Ridge, V2W 1J1; 604-463-7216

This is a must-stop for the salmon fans. Bruce's make a candied salmon that is rumored to be the best in the world. I might have started that rumor, but I'm sure you'll agree. (bruces.ca)

The Firehall Bistro

#104 19237 – 122a Ave., Pitt Meadows, V3Y 2T1; 604-460-7779

The food is flawless, the service impeccable. This is a white-tablecloth, fine-dining experience definitely worth trying. They don't have a website, so you'll have to go old school and call for a reservation.

Foamers' Folly Brewing Co.

19221 – 122a Ave., Pitt Meadows, V3Y 2E9; 604-459-9817

A tasting room with more than 20 choices on tap makes Foamers' Folly a fun place to spend a little time. Kids are allowed in until 9:00 pm, there are board games to play and records to spin (you can channel your inner DJ), and on warm summer nights or hot afternoons you can relax outside on the patio. Pizza, hot dogs, and bar snacks will satisfy your need for food, and if you aren't a beer lover (or you're a minor), you'll be happy to hear that they make a wicked good root beer! (foamersfolly.ca)

The Honeybee Centre

7480 – 176th St., Surrey, V3S 7B1; 604-575-2337

This place always makes me think that if I was still in school, it would be the coolest field trip ever. Everything you ever wanted to know about bees and honey. So much fun! (honeybeecentre.com)

Mission Springs Brewing

7160 Oliver Street, Mission, V2V 6K5; 604-820-1009

One of BC's first craft breweries, Mission Springs has been making delicious beer for over a decade. It's also a pub and a family-friendly restaurant (they even have a kids' menu). You can tour the brewery, sample a flight of beer, or just kick back with a giant plate of nachos and a pint. (missionsprings.ca)

Sugar Patisserie

#103 17767 – 64th Ave., Surrey, V3S 1Z2; 604-574-1551

A little taste of Paris in Surrey. The cases inside Sugar Patisserie are loaded with goodies and will have something to satisfy every sweet tooth. Classic French macarons, croissants, and cookies are easy to eat in the car between tour stops, but if you plan ahead you can order one of owner and pastry chef Caitlin Mayo's signature cakes or tortes. (sugarpatisserie.ca)

Tap Restaurant

#101 15350 – 34th Ave., Surrey, V3S 0T7; 604-536-1954

Great food made with local ingredients, live music, and a phenomenal wine list mean that Tap should be on the top of your list for lunch or dinner when you visit Surrey. (taprestaurant.ca)

Westminster Abbey

34224 Dewdney Trunk Rd., Mission, V2V 4J5; 604-826-8975

Do you know that phrase "serenity now!"? Well, this is where you find it. The trails, the views, the peace—it's incredible. (westminsterabbey.ca)

Fraser Valley
Itineraries & Seasons

Before you decide you want to move to the Fraser Valley permanently, you are probably going to want to see all of it! I'm kidding. Maybe. Or maybe you are on a bit of a "schedule" and want to be a bit more methodical in the planning of your visit. Here are a few recommendations for trips you can easily pull off in a single day, unless like me you are easily distracted!

Brewery Crawl

This tour is going to be a blast! Pile your besties in a car, decide who's driving (and promise them your lifelong appreciation for their sacrifice), and hit the road. Don't forget to throw your clean, empty growlers in the car so you can fill them along the way. Don't own any growlers yet? No big deal—collect them as you visit these awesome breweries.

Stop 1. Central City Brewery, Surrey: it has cider and spirits in addition to beer, making it a great way to start the day.

Stop 2. Trading Post Tasting Room, Langley: their brewery in Langley opens a bit later in the day, so it's a perfect second stop. Snack on some spicy roasted nuts or a little charcuterie while you're there. You're going to need to keep your strength up!

Stop 3. Dead Frog, Langley: check the website for tour times, or if you know when you're going to arrive, you can book your spots in advance. Don't leave without trying their latest seasonal creation. They always have something new happening.

Stop 4. Ravens Brewing, Abbotsford: this is a super-cool spot to try some fun collaborations. They work with other local producers to create things like a Coffee Stout with Old Hand Coffee or a seasonal Strawberry Rhubarb Sour. Order a flight—and good luck deciding what will fill your growler when you leave.

Stop 5. Field House Brewing, Abbotsford: you should also eat here. Chef Bonnie's food is outstanding and you'll need to soak up some of that beer by now! Try the tacos. You're welcome.

Stop 6. Old Yale Brewing, Chilliwack: they're closed on Mondays, so check your calendar to avoid disappointment.

Wineries of the Fraser Valley—well, of Langley!

This is such a fantastic day trip, and you don't even have to leave Langley. Of course, if you're in the mood for a cardio-style wine tour you can leave Langley and head east to Abbotsford to try to fit them all in. (Good luck with that AND I hope you have an awesome designated driver!)

Stop 1. Vista D'oro: Chabby the dog will greet you and, if you're lucky, you'll get to chat with Chef Lee or her handsome husband, Patrick, the winemaker in the tasting room. Don't leave without some of Lee's preserves—you need these in your pantry.

Stop 2. Township 7: pop on their website before you visit, as they often have fun events happening like art shows in the vineyard or live music. The wine is excellent but the hospitality really makes this stop special. You're also very welcome to enjoy your own picnic at one of their tables beside the vines.

Stop 3. Backyard Vineyards: they offer such a great selection of wine for you to try or buy, but please don't leave without the bubbles. It is such a nice treat and so well made, you'll be sorry you didn't buy two.

Stop 4. Domaine de Chaberton is a perfect spot to eat a late lunch or a snack, or just to enjoy a tasting flight. You can sit at a picnic table out front to drink your wine or sip on it while you scarf a chocolate mousse in the bistro (or so I have heard).

Stop 5. Glass House Estate Winery: this new kid on the block at time of writing is as far south as you can go in Langley but so worth spending the extra few minutes you will need to get there. The winery is owned by the de Jong family and the hospitality you will experience there is second to none. They offer live music, painting parties, BBQs with guest chefs (like me), and other special events. Visit their website or Facebook page to check on the latest offerings so you can plan accordingly.

A Family Day Trip

Just to be clear, kids are welcome at ALL of the places I have featured in this book. But some are definitely more fun for the kids than, say, a full day of hanging out at wineries and breweries watching mom and dad play. Regardless of the season, there are so many great things for the family to do—you can almost guarantee the kids will sleep through the entire drive home! The spots I've listed here are year-round options.

Stop 1. Nature's Pickin's, Abbotsford: you can pick up a ton of local food for dinner, watch the goats on the roof, and meet Vicki the cow in the demonstration dairy barn. If you visit in spring, don't miss the tulip festival (abbotsfordtulipfestival.ca).

Stop 2. Maan Farms, Abbotsford: it has an amazing corn maze and pumpkin patch in the fall. You can easily spend a whole day playing in the "critter corral." The kids are going to beg you for another visit, so you should probably buy a season pass on your first visit.

Stop 3. Taves Family Farms, Abbotsford: this is a magical spot, one that really deserves a day to itself so you can do it all! Fire the corn gun, watch them press fresh apple cider, take a pony ride, or fire the pumpkin cannon. Jump till you drop on the pumpkin pillow, tour the petting barns, or conquer the corn maze.

U-Pick or PYO Paradise

It's summer time and the picking is easy! Well, actually it is pretty hard work, but there is definitely a certain satisfaction that comes from getting your hands dirty and channeling your inner farmer. There truly is no better way to enhance your appreciation and understanding of where your food comes from than by harvesting it yourself.

Don't forget your hat, your sunscreen, and your bucket. You'll leave with some delicious fruit that you can jam, can, or freeze and some really great memories to be sure. But the fun isn't restricted to summer; see my suggestions for some fruity fall fun.

SUMMER

Stop 1. Driediger Farms, Langley: have an ice cream after you pick your weight in fresh strawberries. You've earned it.

Stop 2. Krause Berry Farms, Langley: enjoy a corn pizza and pick fresh raspberries. Come back in the evening to watch a movie on their big screen under the stars.

Stop 3. Gojoy, Langley: pick your own fresh goji berries (check the website for availability as they're seasonal). Your fingers will be the most amazing shade of pink when you're done!

FALL

Stop 1. Taves Family Farms, Abbotsford: for the U-pick apples in the fall, there are so many varieties to choose from, the hardest decision you will have to make when you get home is, pie or crumble?

Stop 2. Rondriso, Surrey: pick the perfect pumpkin! You can take a hay ride into the fields and make sure you get exactly what you need to sufficiently terrorize the trick-or-treaters this year!

Foodie Tour

Some say the best way to explore a destination is through your palate. I agree. Experiencing the food produced in any region of the world is one of the best ways to learn about the culture, the environment, the traditions, and the people you meet along the way. Of course, all of the spots profiled in this book will appeal to anyone who has a passion for great local food but there are a few spots that are total game-changers for foodies. Pack your reusable shopping bags and remember to bring an ice chest with ice packs. Trust me, you'll be glad you did.

Stop 1. Well Seasoned gourmet food store, Langley: You are going to need crackers. Lots and lots of crackers. You will find a ton of other tasty bits that you will have a hard time resisting. Check the schedule ahead of time, as there might be a cooking class you want to take later in the day.

Stop 2. Milner Valley Cheese, Langley. You really do need to try the goat gelato and stock up on their fresh and aged chèvres. If you're a lamb lover, ask them if they have any of their farm-raised lamb available.

Stop 3. Blacksmith Bakery, Fort Langley: they make a killer pizza that's perfect for lunch after you've spent a few hours strolling through the antique shops and boutiques in Fort Langley before you continue east.

Stop 4. Nature's Pickin's, Abbotsford: this is hands down the best place to get the freshest assortment of locally grown, seasonal produce any time of year.

Stop 5. The Farm Store at Fraser Valley Specialty Poultry, Yarrow, will satisfy your inner carnivore. Local poultry of every variety, local pork, beef, and lamb fill the fridges and freezers. Ready-to-eat products, local coffee, condiments, and cheese. You're gonna need to get a part-time job when you get home!

Step 6. The Farm House Natural Cheeses, Agassiz: they offer an incredible selection of cow milk and goat milk cheese. You can also fill your bags with fresh eggs, local honey, and even freshly made bread. All you'll need to add is wine and you'll have all you'll need for a truly indulgent few days' eating!

Seasons in the Fraser Valley

You now know, from reading this book, that there is plenty to eat and drink here in the valley at any time of year! But there is so much more to see, visit, and do, too. Here is a quick overview of some of the highlights of each season:

SEASON	REGION	THINGS TO SEE, DO, AND VISIT
Spring	Langley	Giants hockey game (vancouvergiants.com), Stealth lacrosse game (stealthlax.com), or Fort Langley Beer & Food Festival (fortlangley.beer)
	Abbotsford	Tulip Festival (abbotsfordtulipfestival.ca)
	Chilliwack	Barn Burner BBQ (barnburnerbbq.ca)
	Neighbors	Cloverdale Rodeo (cloverdalerodeo.com)
Summer	Langley	Berry picking
	Abbotsford	Abbotsford International Airshow (abbotsfordairshow.com)
	Chilliwack	Swimming at Cultus Lake
	Neighbors	Picnic at a beach or go for a bike ride
Fall	Langley	Cranberry Festival (fortlangley.com), Apple Festival (drbipa.org), or Grave Tales tour (pc.gc.ca/fortlangley)
	Abbotsford	Corn mazes (maanfarms.com; tavesfamilyfarms.com; abbyroadside.com)
	Chilliwack	Reapers Haunted Attraction (reapers.ca) or Garlic & Rockabilly Festival (chilliwackgarlicfestival.ca)
	Neighbors	Pumpkin patch at Rondriso (rondrisofarms.ca/pumpkin-patch)
Winter	Langley	Cooking class at Well Seasoned (wellseasoned.ca) or thrifting in downtown Langley
	Abbotsford	Motorcycle Show at the Tradex (vancouvermotorcycleshow.ca) or BC Hopfest (bchop.ca)
	Chilliwack	Catch a show at the Chilliwack Cultural Centre (chilliwackculturalcentre.ca)
	Neighbors	Outdoor ice skating (if the weather cooperates; it's so much fun and requires hot chocolate!)

Thank You

This book has been a labor of love, one that happened because Robert McCullough understood my passion for the Fraser Valley and shares my belief that good food is best shared with people you care about. Thank you, Robert. I am incredibly grateful for the opportunity you gave me. Lesley Cameron, my Random House "handler," did a great job wrangling this kitten, keeping me focused, on track, and well punctuated—I never would have finished this without you. I am grateful to Lindsay Paterson for her vision and her patience. Special thanks go to my friend and longtime associate, Kathryn (Kay) Slater, whose illustrations and hand-drawn maps are an awesome addition to this book.

I would also like to express my extreme gratitude to Ric Ernst. He brought this book to life with his beautiful photography. Ric's timely retirement meant I had unrestricted access to his talents—he showed up rain or shine and captured my heart through his lens. Special thanks to Renee Blackstone, for your invaluable assistance with the photos and direction. To my Well Seasoned team—Maricor, Sue, Kim, Nicki, Joanne, and Michele—you guys rock. Mari and Sue, recipe testers and food stylists with a vision, you guys are fantastic.

To the farmers, producers, brewmasters, winemakers, and artisans who are featured in this book and to those who aren't—you have my eternal gratitude and respect. Thank you for your generosity and your contributions to the book and to the Fraser Valley. Keep doing what you do—the world needs you! I need you!

And my parents and grandparents, who support me no matter what, who taught me to be a decent human being, to think about other people, to appreciate good food, and to make the time to share a meal—thank you.

Last but by absolutely no means least, thank you to David Gassaway, the love of my life, for encouraging me to pursue my passion every day. It means the world to me—as do you.

Index

People and Places

Recipes and Ingredients

Another way to support local: Get involved with charities like Langley-based TinyKittens.com, who rescue cats like Mason (pictured above).